D1010887

JESUS
God's Gift
of Hope

KAY ARTHUR

HARVEST HOUSE™ PUBLISHERS

EUGENE, OREGON

Cover by Koechel Peterson & Associates, Inc., Minneapolis, Minnesota

JESUS, GOD'S GIFT OF HOPE
Copyright © 2003 by Kay Arthur
Published by Harvest House Publishers
Eugene, OR 97402
www.harvesthousepublishers.com

Library of Congress Cataloging-in-Publication Data

Arthur, Kay, 1933-
    Jesus, God's gift of hope / Kay Arthur.
        p. cm. — (A journey of prayer through the life of Christ) Includes bibliographical references.
    ISBN 0-7369-0644-4
    1. Jesus Christ—Biography—Meditations.   I. Title.
    BT301.3.A78 2003
    242—dc21

03 04 05 06 07 08 09 10 11 / RDC-MS / 10 9 8 7 6 5 4 3 2 1

This is dedicated to all those precious Precept students—men, women, teens, and children—who have given themselves so diligently to the study of God's Word so that they might be pleasing to Him. "Were not our hearts burning within us while He was speaking to us...while He was explaining the Scriptures to us?" (Luke 24:32). You, Beloved of the burning heart, are loved and admired by your servant and friend.

Kay
May 2003

Contents

One

When God Is Silent

Silence. Nothing but silence. God seems far away. You read. You pray. Nothing happens. Or at least you feel that way. You want to draw close to God, but He is beyond your reach. You cannot figure out where God is and why you do not have the intimacy with Him that you long for.

Have you ever been there? I have. It's discouraging, isn't it? You wonder what you've done, why this silence swallows you. At times like these we must remember: God is not silent. He has spoken. Perhaps as I was, you are expecting something—an emotion, a feeling, a sense of His presence, a clear and definite answer to prayer—that God is not going to give you now. But rest, my friend. It will come. In His way. In His perfect timing. Just know that although right now you are not hearing anything, not feeling anything, He's there. God is with you. Don't stop listening for His voice.

Come, my friend. Let's take a journey of prayer together through the days surrounding the birth of the Son of God, the Word made flesh, and see what happens. Let's see how the Spirit moves—what emotions He will stir in us, what tears will come and wash our souls, what heavenly whispers we might hear in the stillness of contemplation. Let's see what insights will delight our minds and clear our thinking, what revelations God will give as He shares His Word with us.

Did you know God's people once endured four hundred years of silence? For four long centuries, no prophet called out the word of the Lord; no one offered exhortation, warning, promises, or reassurance. During this time, Israel was trampled again from the north, this time by Antiochus Epiphanes, a man so despicable he would become the prototype of *the* Antichrist, the man of lawlessness yet to come.

Silence.

A valiant family, the Macabbeans, regained Israel's desecrated temple and consecrated it afresh.

Silence.

In 63 B.C., Pompey fulfilled Daniel's prophecy by conquering the land promised forever to Abraham, Isaac, and Jacob and his descendants.

Silence.

Where was God? Why was He silent? Had He abandoned His people? No, He could not abandon them because He is God, and He keeps His covenants forever. He was silent because He had already warned them of what was coming, but they disregarded His Word. Even so, He was there. God is always there.

Some said, "The Lord has forsaken us. The Lord has forgotten us." But the faithful knew this was impossible, because they knew God. They knew He kept His promises. So they clung to this knowledge even though the heavens seemed as brass.

Then one day, quite unexpectedly, God broke His silence.

The last days, which Isaiah, Daniel, and the other prophets of renown spoke about, had finally dawned, and God was about to speak to His people in a way He had never spoken to them before—through His Son.

*O Beloved Father, You seem so far away. So unreach-
able. So silent. Others speak of hearing Your voice, of
feeling Your presence, of gaining new revelations—but I
don't. I want to, but I don't. Father, I don't want to
conjure up feelings in myself that are not genuine,*

emotions that are of my own making. Frankly, that scares me, for how can I know what is from You? I want reality. But I also want my spirit to be awakened, renewed, refreshed. I long for revival in my heart—a great awakening.

The book of Hebrews says that "God...in these last days has spoken to us in His Son" and that "for this reason we must pay much closer attention to what we have heard, so that we do not drift away from it" (1:1-2; 2:1).

O Lord, the word You spoke through Your prophets was enough to keep some people faithful, steadfast, and true to You, even during four hundred years of silence. I am confident that what You have spoken in the life of Jesus Christ is enough for me today, even when You seem to be silent.

Thank You, thank You, for speaking to me through Your Son. I want to know what You have said in all its depth and clarity. I want to understand it, cling to it. I do not want to drift away. As I take this journey of prayer through the birth and early life of your Son, please speak afresh to my heart. May Your words become palpable to me, stimulating and sharpening my spiritual senses. Cause me to love You again with the same fresh excitement I experienced when I first came to know You. Cause me to love You with that settled comfort that comes when love has grown and matured through the years and trials shared together.

This is what I ask in the name of Your Son, the Lord Jesus Christ.

Luke
1:5-17

In the days of Herod, king of Judea, there was a priest named Zacharias, of the division of Abijah; and he had a wife from the daughters of Aaron, and her name was Elizabeth. They were both righteous in the sight of God, walking blamelessly in all the commandments and requirements of the Lord. But they had no child, because Elizabeth was barren, and they were both advanced in years.

Now it happened that while he was performing his priestly service before God in the appointed order of his division, according to the custom of the priestly office, he was chosen by lot to enter the temple of the Lord and burn incense. And the whole multitude of the people were in prayer outside at the hour of the incense offering.

And an angel of the Lord appeared to him, standing to the right of the altar of incense. Zacharias was troubled when he saw the angel, and fear gripped him. But the angel said to him, "Do not be afraid, Zacharias, for your petition has been heard, and your wife Elizabeth will bear you a son, and you will give him the name John. You will have joy and gladness, and many will rejoice at his birth. For he will be great in the sight of the Lord, and he will drink no wine or liquor; and he will be filled with the Holy Spirit while yet in his mother's womb. And he will turn many of the sons of Israel back to the Lord their God. It is he who will go as a forerunner before Him in the spirit and power of Elijah, TO TURN THE HEARTS OF THE FATHERS BACK TO THE CHILDREN, and the disobedient to the attitude of the righteous; so as to make ready a people prepared for the Lord."

Two

When You Are Weary of Waiting

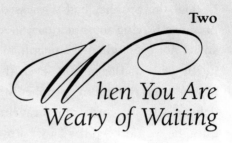

$\mathcal{I}$t happened in the sanctuary. Isn't that usually where we hear God's voice most clearly? In the place where we are alone, worshiping God, honoring Him as God by giving Him a portion of the day He has given us?

There in the sanctuary, four hundred years of silence came to an end. But not with trumpets, nor with fanfare, nor with crackling lightning and booming claps of thunder that make bodies jump and hearts race.

Zacharias, a priest of the division of Abijah, was chosen by lot to burn incense in the temple of the Lord as prescribed by the Torah. When he entered the temple at the hour of the incense offering, the people gathered for prayer outside this imposing structure aggrandized by Herod the Great, who was so named for the showy buildings he loved to erect.

Inside, a veil separated Zacharias from the Holy of Holies, but there was no Shekinah glory on the other side. Not quite six hundred years earlier, just before the Babylonian invasion, Ezekiel the prophet had witnessed the holy cloud of God's presence leaving the sanctuary. God's form had not returned since, not even when the people meagerly rebuilt the temple in the days of Haggai. But even though the holy cloud was absent, even though the prophet Malachi had been the last to deliver a fresh word from heaven, Zacharias would do his duty; he would keep the Law.

The holy fire was in the incense pan when Zacharias suddenly realized he was not alone. Only one priest was to perform this ritual, the Law declared, not two. But there to the right of the altar stood another. Fear gripped Zacharias as the deafening silence of four hundred years was broken by the angel of the Lord. Let us read his words again:

> Do not be afraid, Zacharias, for your petition has been heard, and your wife Elizabeth will bear you a son, and you will give him the name John. You will have joy and gladness, and many will rejoice at his birth. For he will be great in the sight of the Lord, and he will drink no wine or liquor; and he will be filled with the Holy Spirit while yet in his mother's womb. And he will turn back many of the sons of Israel to the Lord their God.
>
> It is he who will go as a forerunner before Him in the spirit and power of Elijah, TO TURN THE

HEARTS OF THE FATHERS BACK TO THE CHILDREN, and
the disobedient to the attitude of the righteous; so
as to make ready a people prepared for the Lord
(Luke 1:13-17).

For years, Zacharias and Elizabeth had petitioned God for
a child. Month after month, year after year, the shame of
"barren Elizabeth" had grown. Elizabeth and Zacharias both
knew that the Lord opens and shuts the womb. They had
petitioned Him, yet He remained silent. The gift of a child was
not impossible for God. "Nothing is too difficult for You,"
Jeremiah had written (Jeremiah 32:17). Had He not heard?
Did He not care? Why? Why would He not give them a child?
Children had been part of God's plan since the garden of
Eden!

The years passed, and their hope waned until it was gone,
as dead now as Elizabeth's womb. Women Elizabeth's age did
not bear children.

But now! Now God is ready to speak, after all these years of
silence! And what He has to say, He will say to one man. One
man and his wife. A couple who—despite God's silence,
despite unanswered prayer, despite disgrace (Luke 1:25)—had
remained "righteous in the sight of God, walking blamelessly
in all the commandments and requirements of the Lord" (1:6).

Can you, my friend, understand how they felt? Maybe you are or have been where Elizabeth and Zacharias were before God broke His silence. Maybe all seems hopeless to you. Perhaps God in His silence has said no, and you can not understand why because He is God and nothing is too difficult for Him.

I would not dare to trample on God's holy ground and tell you why He has not answered your prayer. I do not know why He has kept silent. But, dear one, I would bring you hope with this account of Elizabeth and Zacharias. For what God was about to do for them was far greater than they ever could have imagined in the years they waited upon God, enduring testing, being proven, and continuing in righteousness even when God did not do what they asked of Him.

The son that Elizabeth would bear would be the fulfillment of God's last promises through the prophet Malachi. Their son—*their son*—would be Messiah's forerunner. He—*their son; catch the absolute wonder of it all!*—would make ready a people prepared for the Lord! Who could have ever dreamed such a thing?

Oh, stay, Beloved, stay in the sanctuary. Stay close to God. You never know when He is going to speak, or what He is going to say.

When You Are Weary of Waiting

O Father, regardless of what You say, regardless of whether You answer my cries, I want to be like Zacharias and Elizabeth. Even if I feel disgraced by Your silence, even if I told others I was sure You would answer, even if You never do what I think is best, I want to remember, You are God.

Your way, Your timing, is perfect. Your sight is so much clearer than mine, for You, my Alpha and Omega, know the beginning from the end. Your ways are so much higher than mine, Your thoughts so much greater than mine.

Help me to worship You correctly by remembering this and by living as You would have me live, regardless of Your silence, regardless of everything and anything. May I also remember that when You are ready to move, my age will make no difference in the scope of Your plan. As You did with Sarah and Abraham, as You did with Zacharias and Elizabeth, You can move mightily among the old as well as the young. My times are in Your hands.

Thank You, Father, for those hands, which You, in Your infinite love for mankind—for me—stretched out wide and let others impale.

I love You, Father, not for what You do, but for Who You are—my God.

Luke 1:26-37

Now in the sixth month the angel Gabriel was sent from God to a city in Galilee called Nazareth, to a virgin engaged to a man whose name was Joseph, of the descendants of David; and the virgin's name was Mary. And coming in, he said to her, "Greetings, favored one! The Lord is with you." But she was greatly troubled at this statement, and kept pondering what kind of salutation this was.

The angel said to her, "Do not be afraid, Mary; for you have found favor with God. And behold, you will conceive in your womb and bear a son, and you shall name Him Jesus. He will be great and will be called the Son of the Most High; and the Lord God will give Him the throne of His father David; and He will reign over the house of Jacob forever; and His kingdom will have no end." Mary said to the angel, "How can this be, since I am a virgin?" The angel answered and said to her, "The Holy Spirit will come upon you, and the power of the Most High will overshadow you; and for that reason the holy Child shall be called the Son of God. And behold, even your relative Elizabeth has also conceived a son in her old age; and she who was called barren is now in her sixth month. For nothing will be impossible with God."

Three

*N*othing—Absolutely Nothing—Is Impossible with God!

*I*t seemed impossible. *Inconceivable* in the truest sense of the word. No virgin could conceive a child! Yet the angel of the Lord explained how it would happen: The Holy Spirit would come upon Mary, and the power of the Most High would overshadow her, and the holy Child would be called the Son of God. The angel Gabriel assured Mary that "nothing will be impossible with God" (Luke 1:37). The word for "nothing" in this scripture is literally "not any word." Not any word of God's is ever void of power. God had ordained it. The word had been spoken, the message delivered.

Mary—the virgin engaged to Joseph—would give birth to the only begotten Son of God.

Who was this woman? Do you ever wonder why Mary, of all the women on the face of the earth, was chosen by God for the unique, never-to-be-repeated experience of giving birth to the Son of God? How did she, of all the daughters of Israel, find such favor with God?

The Word of God gives us no explanation. It simply introduces us to Mary, a human being just like you and me in need of redemption. God's focus is not on Mary's history, except that she is a virgin. Rather, He is concerned that we note the response of this woman, whom generations would count blessed beyond all other women because of the favor God bestowed on her.

Oh, to know the favor of God! To be pleasing to Him! What a privilege to be the person chosen by God for the honor of bearing His Son in your body! In a sense, however, isn't that what we have the honor of doing when we believe God's message, His glorious gospel, and receive Jesus Christ as our Lord and Savior? Isn't that what happens when our bodies become His temple (1 Corinthians 3:17; 6:19)?

Granted, Mary's experience was unique among women. As I think about it, however, I realize how blessed we believers are among all mankind to be indwelt by the Son of God through the power of the Holy Spirit. Christ—the long-awaited Messiah, the promised One—is in us! *Christ in us,* the hope of glory (Colossians 1:27)!

As I apply this incredible reality to my own condition on the day of my salvation, I am caught up in the wonder of it all:

Mary didn't know how she could bear the Son of God because she was a virgin (Luke 1:34).

I didn't know how I could be indwelt by the Son of God because I was chief among sinners.

Mary had known no man.

I was a fornicator—a woman who had known many men.

Mary was a descendant of David.

I was a Gentile, without God and without hope, a stranger to the covenants of promise (Ephesians 2:11-13).

Yet He whom Mary bore, I would someday bear. Think of it! My body would become the temple of the living God! Mary would be blessed among women, and I am blessed among women. You, too, my brothers and sisters, are blessed among humankind.

If you would have explained this plan of God to me years ago, I would have thought, *How ridiculous! Impossible!* But then, I was blind to truth. That I should ever become a woman of God, a daughter of the Almighty, a child of the sovereign ruler of the universe, was impossible except for one thing:

No word of God is void of power.

What God speaks will happen; what He says will come to pass. Ephesians 1:3-4 says that God chose me in Christ before the foundation of the world. God chose you, too. Neither heaven nor hell could stop Him from gathering us to Himself.

God had spoken—and God cannot lie nor go back on what He promises.

What was about to happen to Mary would fulfill the promise God made to two miserable people, Adam and Eve, who had plummeted all mankind into a state of sin. The woman would have "a seed" that would bruise the head of the serpent of old, the devil and Satan (Genesis 3:15, Revelation 12:9; 20:2). Mary would fulfill the promise made through the prophet Isaiah: "Behold, a virgin will be with child and bear a son, and she will call His name Immanuel" (Isaiah 7:14). Immanuel means "God with us"!

> For a child will be born to us, a son will be given to us;
> And the government will rest on His shoulders;
> And His name will be called Wonderful Counselor, Mighty God,
> Eternal Father, Prince of Peace.
> There will be no end to the increase of His government or of peace,
> On the throne of David and over his kingdom,
> To establish it and to uphold it with justice and righteousness
> From then on and forevermore.
> The zeal of the LORD of hosts will accomplish this (Isaiah 9:6-7).

God would bring it to pass—in His time. Mary's child would be given to us, and the government of our lives would rest no longer on our shoulders but on His! All this would be accomplished by the zeal of Jehovah Sabaoth—the Lord of hosts—through the power of the Holy Spirit.

Mary heard the good news. The long-awaited Messiah was coming, and she, a young girl living in Nazareth, promised in marriage to a man named Joseph who was also of the house of David, would give birth to Him. God would bring it to pass. That was all Mary needed to know. Mary didn't ask how all this would work in relationship to Joseph,

or how to explain her situation to him,

or what they would tell friends and family,

or how she would be received by others who learned she was pregnant before the wedding.

Instead, she simply said, "Behold, the bondslave of the Lord; be it done to me according to your word" (Luke 1:38).

God could be trusted.

God *would* be trusted.

And this, Beloved, is Mary's example to us. Mary believed, and God brought it to pass.

And what about us? Will we believe all God says and trust Him to bring it to pass in His time, in His way? With convicting power, the Holy Spirit has told us we need to be born again, to believe in Jesus Christ, that we might have eternal life. The mystery of how it all takes place remains, but when we say, "May it be done to me according to Your word," or, "I believe, I accept, I trust. Do with me as You please, for You are God," He will bring it to pass. Jesus takes up residence within us, and our bodies become the temple of the Holy Spirit because nothing is impossible with God.

O Father, I stand in awe that You looked down on me with such favor and, in the fullness of time, sent Your Son to be born of a woman, to become flesh and blood like me. Because of Your great love, I have a Savior who knows my weakness, who has been tempted in all things as I have, yet without sin (Hebrews 4:15). For this reason He was able to die in my place, being made sin for me and for all mankind (2 Corinthians 5:21).

Thank You for loving me, for calling me "Beloved" when nothing about me was lovely, and for giving me a Savior. Thank You for Your incomprehensible mercy, kindness, and grace. Truly, nothing is impossible for You.

Precious Lord, as Mary submitted herself to You, may I, too, submit. As she gave birth to Your Son, willing to endure the scorn and shame of those who didn't under-stand, may I also bear Him before others in such a way that all might see Him, see His works of grace, see His power to transform sinners into saints. And Father, if men scorn me, reject me, blaspheme my character, or wrongly accuse me, may I understand that they do so simply because they do not know You. May their ignorance not prevent me from giving Jesus to the world.

Luke
1:39-45

Now at this time Mary arose and went in a hurry to the hill country, to a city of Judah, and entered the house of Zacharias and greeted Elizabeth. When Elizabeth heard Mary's greeting, the baby leaped in her womb; and Elizabeth was filled with the Holy Spirit.

And she cried out with a loud voice and said, "Blessed are you among women, and blessed is the fruit of your womb! And how has it happened to me, that the mother of my Lord would come to me? For behold, when the sound of your greeting reached my ears, the baby leaped in my womb for joy. And blessed is she who believed that there would be a fulfillment of what had been spoken to her by the Lord."

Four

Blessed Are Those Who Believe

$\mathcal{D}$o you sometimes find it hard to believe God, especially when your circumstances seem so impossible? Most of us wrestle with this. Yet God knows, and He graciously speaks strength to the weakness of our faith.

As soon as the angel left Mary, she hurried to the home of Zacharias and Elizabeth, her relatives. The angel had told Mary that Elizabeth had also conceived a child even though she was barren.

When Mary entered Elizabeth's home, God again confirmed His pleasure in the mother of our Lord. He so filled Elizabeth with His Spirit that she cried out loudly. Mary couldn't miss a word! Can you hear Elizabeth?

> Blessed are you among women, and blessed is
> the fruit of your womb. And how has it happened
> to me, that the mother of my Lord would come to

me? For behold, when the sound of your greeting
reached my ears, the baby leaped in my womb for
joy. And blessed is she who believed that there
would be a fulfillment of what had been spoken to
her by the Lord (Luke 1:42-45).

"Blessed is she who believed." As I said, it's hard to believe
at times, isn't it? Hard to cling to God, to His Word, to His
promises, especially when their fulfillment seems humanly
impossible. What God told Mary through the angel was so
humanly impossible that one could not help but wonder how
it would ever come to pass.

I'm sure, Beloved, that you have found yourself in situations fraught with impossibility, situations in which despair
hovers over you like a black storm cloud, eclipsing any warm
glimmer of hope. Thunder claps its hands. You wonder if the
sun will ever shine again. You shudder in the chill of its
absence; you wrap your arms more tightly about yourself. You
feel so alone, beaten down as the wind of hopelessness whips
around your body. Sometimes the gusts are so strong that you
lose your balance and wonder if you will topple over the cliff
of despair. The wind whips through your mind, making it
tumble again and again past your weaknesses, your failures,
your impotence. It howls down a hundred corridors of doubt,

fear, discouragement, possibilities, tragedies, failure, and inadequacies.

And when you come to the realization of your total impotence to calm the storm, you cry out in fear and run to God. Slowly, gently, He draws you to Himself, into the wonder of His being, into the strength of His attributes, and then He wraps you in the soft, warm blanket of His promises. At that point you can scream, yell, struggle, and run away again, forgetting that you can't solve this problem yourself, or you can snuggle down in the everlasting arms, resting in the fact that He is God, and nothing is impossible with Him.

Mary was blessed simply because she believed God. She took Him at His Word and left the "fulfillment of what had been spoken to her by the Lord" to Him. And we, Beloved, must do the same.

Faith is the bedrock of all of life—the solid foundation that not only wins the favor of God but also keeps us anchored through the inevitable challenges and difficulties of life. God tells us in the book of Hebrews that without faith it is impossible to please God. Those who come to Him must first and foremost believe that He is God, and second, believe that He is a rewarder of those who seek Him (Hebrews 11:6).

How did Mary express her faith? Listen to what the Common Book of Prayer refers to as the "Magnificat," and stand in awe of Mary's understanding of God:

Jesus, God's Gift of Hope

My soul exalts the Lord,

And my spirit has rejoiced in God my Savior.

For He has had regard for the humble state of His
bondslave;

For behold, from this time on all generations will
count me blessed.

For the Mighty One has done great things for me;

And holy is His name.

AND HIS MERCY IS UPON GENERATION AFTER GENERA-
TION

TOWARD THOSE WHO FEAR HIM.

He has done mighty deeds with His arm;

He has scattered those who were proud in the
thoughts of their heart.

He has brought down rulers from their thrones,

And has exalted those who were humble.

HE HAS FILLED THE HUNGRY WITH GOOD THINGS;

And sent away the rich empty-handed.

He has given help to Israel His servant,

In remembrance of His mercy,

As He spoke to our fathers,

To Abraham and his offspring forever (Luke
1:46-55).

"Magnificat" is the Latin translation of the first word of Mary's song. The Greek word, *megalynei*, means "to enlarge." And what is to be enlarged? It is the greatness of our Lord, so beautifully illuminated by Mary's words. Mary exalted the Lord—she literally "made Him great" in her soul, her mind, her will, her emotions, her intellect. She focused all her being on the greatness of God.

What an example Mary is to us when we are confronted with an issue of faith. Her spirit rejoiced in God her Savior. The One born of her would be *her* Savior. Mary knew her sinfulness, her impotence, her need of Someone who would save her from her sins. And she knew His mercy was available to all who would fear Him.

Mary stood in awe of the favor God had bestowed upon one as lowly as she was. In this one act of choosing someone of her low station, God dashed the proud. He brought down rulers from their lofty thrones of power, and He lifted up those who were humble. The rich who thought they had everything went away empty-handed, and those who hungered, well aware of their lowliness, were filled with good things from the very hand of the Most High God, whose throne and dominion is above all.

The fullness of time had come. The despised and oppressed of Israel were about to receive God's help because of a covenant promise He made to Abraham and his seed forever.

No word of God is void of power.

Nothing is impossible with Him.

Blessed are those who believe.

Mary believed and was blessed. She proclaimed her belief and stood in awe of her Lord. Will you, Beloved, also believe and be blessed by God as a result? Will you cling to His promises, knowing that He will fulfill those things spoken to you in His Word?

Indeed, the storm *will* pass, the darkness *will* fade, and the sun *will* shine because God is God, and He rewards those who seek Him.

O Holy Father, how I thank You that You are the Mighty One, the God of all mercies. Thank You for meeting me in my hunger, my humility, my total dependence upon You. Truly my heart rejoices in God my Savior! I would be forever lost without You, doomed to the fruit of my ways, if You had not lovingly regarded my desperate condition.

O blessed Father, I believe; please help my unbelief (Mark 9:23-24). May I long to know You in the fullness of Your character as Mary knew You. May I learn Your Word and then remember that no word of Yours—nothing—is impossible with You. You watch over Your Word to perform it because You are a God who is faithful (Romans 4:20-21).

Help me—remind me—to walk in faith in the light of Your Word moment by moment, situation by situation, storm by storm. I believe that You are God and that You reward those who seek You. Whatever my situation, whatever my circumstance, may I look to You, cry out to You, and remember that You will supply all my needs according to Your riches in glory (Philippians 4:19) through the One who was conceived of the Holy Spirit and born of Mary—my Savior at all times, in all ways, for ever and ever. Amen.

Luke
1:18-25

Now the birth of Jesus Christ was as follows: when His mother Mary had been betrothed to Joseph, before they came together she was found to be with child by the Holy Spirit. And Joseph her husband, being a righteous man and not wanting to disgrace her, planned to send her away secretly. But when he had considered this, behold, an angel of the Lord appeared to him in a dream, saying, "Joseph, son of David, do not be afraid to take Mary as your wife; for the Child who has been conceived in her is of the Holy Spirit. She will bear a Son; and you shall call His name Jesus, for He will save His people from their sins." Now all this took place to fulfill what was spoken by the Lord through the prophet: "BEHOLD, THE VIRGIN SHALL BE WITH CHILD AND SHALL BEAR A SON, AND THEY SHALL CALL HIS NAME IMMANUEL," which translated means, "GOD WITH US." And Joseph awoke from his sleep and did as the angel of the Lord commanded him, and took Mary as his wife, but kept her a virgin until she gave birth to a Son; and he called His name Jesus.

he Power of Practiced Character

And he "kept her a virgin." That is quite a statement, isn't it? It is so rare these days, so noble, to love someone, to desire someone, and yet to restrain passion!

But then Joseph was "a righteous man."

Joseph didn't seem to know of Mary's pregnancy until at least three months after the angel appeared to her and told her that she would give birth to the Son of God. Mary had gone in haste to the hill country of Judah, and she didn't return from their home until after about three months (Luke 1:39,56).

This righteous man must have been devastated to learn that the woman he was about to marry carried a child who wasn't his. And yet, who better than a righteous man to deal with something like this? If you have determined to live righteously, according to the precepts of God, then when disconcerting news comes, your acquired discipline—your ability to restrain passion and temper—will help you control life's contingencies rather than be controlled by them. Practiced character can harness and rein in tears, pain, sorrow, disappointment, anger, and bitterness of soul.

Because Joseph was a righteous man, he determined to deal with Mary's pregnancy in a way that would not bring her even greater shame. He could have had her stoned—dragged before the elders of Israel and put to death according to the Law. Like all marriage covenants of that time, a betrothal could be broken if the woman was found to be unclean. Certainly Mary's pregnancy testified to this. Yet Joseph's righteousness restrained him. Considering all his options according to the Word of God and the traditions of the times, Joseph decided to send Mary away secretly. Rather than vindicating himself and shaming her publicly, he would simply divorce her privately.

A righteous man is never alone. God is always with him. The righteous are never forsaken.

In the midst of Joseph's turmoil, an angel came to him, just as one had come to Mary to tell her that she had been chosen to bear the Son of God. Only this time the angel appeared to Joseph in a dream, saying,

> Joseph, son of David, do not be afraid to take
> Mary as your wife; for the Child who has been

conceived in her is of the Holy Spirit. She will bear
a Son; and you shall call His name Jesus, for He
will save His people from their sins (Matthew
1:20-21).

Was it true? Could it be? This was a child conceived by the
Spirit of God?

Did Joseph's mind race back through the Word of God,
seeking confirmation, searching the words of the prophet to
see if anything like this had been promised? That a virgin
would have a child? That God would have a son?

Matthew tells us that

all this took place to fulfill what was spoken by the
Lord through the prophet: "BEHOLD, THE VIRGIN
SHALL BE WITH CHILD AND SHALL BEAR A SON, AND
THEY SHALL CALL HIS NAME IMMANUEL," which trans-
lated means, "GOD WITH US" (verses 22-23).

God would dwell with man! God would become a man!
The One born of Joseph's betrothed would save God's people
from their sins! That's why he, Joseph, was to name Him
Jesus! The long-awaited Messiah would finally come—but as
a babe born of a virgin! Deity would confine Himself to the
womb of a woman, wrap Himself up in the total impotence of

a baby. Joseph and Mary would raise the Son of God! The Savior of the world! The hope of all ages!

Unbelievable!

Yet Joseph, the righteous man, believed.

> And Joseph awoke from his sleep and did as the angel of the Lord commanded him, and took Mary as his wife, but kept her a virgin until she gave birth to a Son; and he called His name Jesus (verses 24-25).

Joseph married Mary, but for the remainder of her pregnancy, he restrained himself—he "kept her a virgin" until the Son of God was born.

The time would come when Joseph could fulfill his desires and know the unique pleasure of a wife. And he would know this pleasure, in all the fullness of its beauty, in the wonder of its ecstasy. Yet he would know it with a clear conscience, for Joseph would know his wife in the timing of God. He would know her in the exquisite purity and unabashed delight of uncovering the nakedness of the one woman who belonged to God and to him—the woman to whom he alone belonged.

No thoughts of others, no memories of past liaisons would sully his mind, for Joseph was a righteous man. He was a righteous man who kept his wife a virgin until he had God's blessing—the blessing of obedience, the blessing that belongs to the righteous, the blessing that belongs to those who have restrained passions and kept a clear conscience before God and man.

O Father, how You have spoken through a man mentioned so little in Your Word. Yet to this man You gave the task of being an earthly father to Your Son.

My heart is touched by what I have learned about Joseph. And I am smitten by desire—the desire to be righteous, the desire to be a person whom You can trust to listen to You, the desire to hear Your voice and do Your will. I want to restrain my passions, my ambitions, and bring them into line with the clear teachings of Your Word.

O Father, I know that Your heart grieves over the impurity of heart and mind that is so blatant in our world. We do not fear You; we do not honor Your commandments. We are so focused on ourselves, our wants, our desires. We do not restrain our passions. We want what we want when we want it, and consequently we move out of Your will. We insist on our timetable rather than Yours so that we can have our flesh's desires now, our way. In the process we have so messed up our lives, the lives of others, the society we live in. How desperately we need a Savior—Your Son—who will save us from ourselves, from our sins.

O Father, I thank You for the righteous man and the righteous woman whom You could trust to bring us Your Son. I thank You that they listened to You, trusted You, and obeyed You.

May I now live righteously in the midst of this crooked and perverse generation, holding forth the Word of Life by walking in Christ's light and His power, the power that has freed me from sin's power.

I ask this for Your glory and my good, in the name of the One You sent, Immanuel.

Luke
1:57-66

Now the time had come for Elizabeth to give birth, and she gave birth to a son. Her neighbors and her relatives heard that the Lord had displayed His great mercy toward her; and they were rejoicing with her.

And it happened that on the eighth day they came to circumcise the child, and they were going to call him Zacharias, after his father. But his mother answered and said, "No indeed; but he shall be called John." And they said to her, "There is no one among your relatives who is called by that name." And they made signs to his father, as to what he wanted him called. And he asked for a tablet and wrote as follows, "His name is John." And they were all astonished. And at once his mouth was opened and his tongue loosed, and he began to speak in praise of God. Fear came on all those living around them; and all these matters were being talked about in all the hill country of Judea. And all who heard them kept them in mind, saying, "What then will this child turn out to be?" For the hand of the Lord was certainly with him.

ave Me and I Will Be Saved!"

$\mathscr{O}$ God, if You don't help me, if You don't rescue me, then all is lost!"

Have you ever uttered words like these? We all come to a time when we are brought face-to-face with our total impotence. You may not have encountered it yet, but the day will come, the day when you cannot rescue yourself. Though you try as hard as you can, you cannot extricate yourself from the situation, from the circumstance that overwhelms you. The situation is too grave,

   too bleak,

      too dark.

The trouble is beyond your control, beyond the power of mortal man.

And you know it. You have done all you can, and yet your best efforts are not enough. You cannot deliver yourself.

Maybe your trouble is a sentence of death.

Maybe it is someone who has risen up as your enemy.

Maybe it is a bondage to an overwhelming craving that you cannot shake.

Maybe it is the tormenting anguish of a life of failure or the rotting harvest of a life of disobedience, which God calls sin.

Whatever it may be, Beloved, do you realize God has raised up a horn of salvation for you?

Are you aware that you can know, that you can *experience*, the peace of God that surpasses all understanding?

He has, and you can. Our salvation is possible because of what He has accomplished for you and for me.

Come, dear one, you do not need to sit in the despair of darkness or in the gloom of the shadow of death. You can cry, "Save me, O God, and I will be saved." Let's open the record books and discover what has been wrought on our behalf: the redemption of our eternal lives.

God's astounding gift for us is recorded in Zacharias' prophecy, which was given on the occasion of his son's circumcision, eight days after his birth. Let's study its context.

When Elizabeth gave birth to their son, she created quite a stir in the hill country of Judah. Apparently, in her barrenness dear Elizabeth had kept herself in seclusion, but not any longer. This elderly barren woman finally bore a son!

When her neighbors and her relatives heard that the Lord had displayed His great mercy toward her, they rejoiced with her. Little did they know what would happen eight days later when the time came to circumcise the child.

Circumcising and naming the baby was truly a community affair.

> They were going to call him Zacharias, after his father. But his mother answered and said, "No indeed; but he shall be called John." And they said to her, "There is no one among your relatives who is called by that name." And they made signs to his father, as to what he wanted him called (Luke 1:59-62).

Elizabeth may have been in seclusion, but all knew that with an untoward turn of events nine months or more earlier, Zacharias had lost his ability to speak. Whether they also thought of him as deaf or he really was, we don't know. The Scriptures simply tell us that suddenly they were protesting to him in sign language.

> And he asked for a tablet and wrote as follows, "His name is John." And they were all astonished (verse 63).

Then it happened. The words came. Words you and I—and over two millennia of generations—need to hear, for at once his mouth was opened and his tongue loosed, and he began to speak in praise of God. Fear came on all those living around them; and all these matters were being talked about in all the hill country of Judea. And all who heard them kept them in mind, saying, "What then will this child turn out to be?" For the hand of the Lord was certainly with him (verses 64-66).

What were Zacharias' words, and where did they come from?

God does not leave us in doubt, nor does He give us over to speculation. Instead, God assures us that the words Zacharias spoke were His very own, spoken through His servant.

God's message to you and to me, this word from heaven, is preserved in Scripture because we desperately need to know and understand it. Listen with your heart as well as your mind, for these words are laden with peace and assurance.

Such peace and assurance cannot be secured by any means except by understanding that God's Word is truth.

This is God's Word, the Bible.

Unsullied.

Untainted.

When embraced in faith, the truth of the Word will shine in your darkness, dispel the shadow of death, quell the threats of your enemies, and give you all that is rightfully yours when you receive forgiveness for your sin.

Zacharias, "filled with the Holy Spirit…prophesied, saying:"

> Blessed be the Lord God of Israel,
> For He has visited us and accomplished redemp-
>   tion for His people,
> And has raised up a horn of salvation for us
> In the house of David His servant—
> As He spoke by the mouth of His holy prophets
>   from of old—
> Salvation FROM OUR ENEMIES,
> And FROM THE HAND OF ALL WHO HATE US;
> To show mercy toward our fathers,
> And to remember His holy covenant,
> The oath which He swore to Abraham our father,
> To grant us that we, being rescued from the hand
>   of our enemies,
> Might serve Him without fear,
> In holiness and righteousness before Him all our
>   days.
> And you, child, will be called the prophet of the
>   Most High;
> For you will go on BEFORE THE LORD TO PREPARE HIS
>   WAYS;

> To give to His people the knowledge of salvation
> By the forgiveness of their sins,
> Because of the tender mercy of our God,
> With which the Sunrise from on high will visit us,
> TO SHINE UPON THOSE WHO SIT IN DARKNESS AND THE
> SHADOW OF DEATH,
> To guide our feet into the way of peace (Luke
> 1:67-79).

Here, Beloved, is the way of peace. Zacharias' prophecy does not dwell on John, the son just born to him. Rather, it focuses on the One whom John will proclaim as he goes before Messiah to prepare His way.

The One at the heart of this prophecy is

- the horn of salvation, raised up by God Himself in the house of His servant David

- the Sunrise from on high, who has visited us and shone upon those who sit in darkness and the shadow of death, to guide us into the way of peace

- the Son of God, the Lord Jesus Christ

In the Scriptures, "horn" is synonymous with "power." Jesus, the One whom John would proclaim, would be the power of salvation, the only salvation that would deliver God's people from their enemies and from all who hated them.

At long last, the Redeemer, the personification of the mercy of God, would come. The time had come for the birth of the Seed of Abraham—the One through whom all the nations of the earth would be blessed. God had not forgotten His promise (Genesis 12:1-3).

The fulfillment of His covenant was about to come to pass.

Mankind had awaited this moment since Adam and Eve's fateful disobedience in the Garden of Eden. At long last, the fears of all people would be dispelled because salvation was assured and secured in the birth of Messiah. The Lamb who would take away the sins of the world was about to be born. And through His work of salvation, a life of holiness and righteousness would now be possible.

The child Zacharias and Elizabeth had just named John would prepare the hearts of the people to receive this good news. The eight-day-old lad they had just circumcised in obedience to the Law of God would introduce God's people to the One who would inaugurate the New Covenant of the grace of God, the One who would bring forgiveness of sins. Those who sat in the shadow of death would no longer have to fear it because death's power would finally be broken through Jesus' birth, death, burial, and resurrection. John would guide God's people into the way of peace as he introduced them to the Prince of Peace.

Have you listened with your heart to God's message delivered through Zacharias? Have you stored it in your mind that you might recall His words as the cure for your troubled heart?

If so, the sentence of death that you are facing is not a sentence of death at all; rather, it is merely a notice of your pending promotion to eternal life.

I remember when my dear brothers Bill Bright, the founder of Campus Crusade for Christ, and Brandt Gustavson, the president of the National Religious Broadcasters, both colleagues of mine, received their sentences of death in 2001. Bill was told his pulmonary fibrosis would prove fatal, and Brandt learned he would die of cancer of the liver and pancreas. Bill could not be told how long he had to live; Brandt could expect two months.

Yet both walked through the shadow of death with a peace that truly surpassed all human understanding.

Peace was theirs because their sins had been forgiven. They knew the horn of their salvation. They experienced the tender mercy of God. And both accomplished their desire, which was to show people how to die in the same way they had taught people, through a lifetime of service to God, how to live. Both men wanted

> To give to His people the knowledge of salva-
> tion
> By the forgiveness of their sins,
> Because of the tender mercy of our God,
> With which the Sunrise from on high shall visit
> us,
> TO SHINE UPON THOSE WHO SIT IN DARKNESS AND THE
> SHADOW OF DEATH,
> To guide our feet into the way of peace (Luke
> 1:77-79).

In the next chapter I will continue this discussion of how God has delivered us from our troubles, but now we must pause here, my friend, for you must have the opportunity to know for certain that you are truly saved and have forgiveness of sins.

Truly saved—saved from eternal separation from God and from man. Saved from the lake of fire, the place where the worm does not die and the fire is not quenched, the place created by God for the devil and his angels (Matthew 25:41; Mark 9:43-44).

Truly saved—saved to live in the presence of God and His people for ever and ever. Saved to bask in the eternal light of the Light of the world (John 17:3). Saved to experience the power of salvation—freedom not only from the penalty of sin but also from its power in this life and in the life to come (Romans 6:4-9). Salvation from your enemies (Luke 1:71).

Of all the prayers you have prayed on our journey so far, the one below is most important. For if you are not saved, then all the other prayers are meaningless if you refuse to come to Him His way—through His Son.

There is no other way. You cannot be good enough, you cannot do enough good deeds, you cannot compare yourself to others and claim the right of heaven. No, instead you must see your own sin, your own wretchedness, and your own impotence to save yourself. This is the only way to make yourself acceptable to God. You must bow before God in poverty of spirit and ask Him in His mercy to save you...and He will.

⁕⁓•

O God, I long to call You "Father" in the truest sense of the word. I want to become Your child, adopted into Your family, born again of the Spirit of God. I want to become a new creation with all things in the past, truly past. Gone. Never to be mentioned again (John 1:12; 3:3; Romans 8:15-17; 2 Corinthians 5:17).

I thank You now for bringing me into Your family, for forgiving me for all my sins—past, present, and future. I thank You that I also have assurance of forgiveness (*John 8:34-36*).

Thank You for Your promise in Hebrews 13:5-6: You will never leave me nor forsake me. I thank You that I can boldly say, "The Lord is my helper—I will not fear what man will do to me." And thank You for the promise that You will complete the good work of salvation You have begun in me (Philippians 1:6) and that no one can pluck me out of Your hand (*John 10:27-28*).

Lord, thank You for the gift of eternal life. Now, help me to grow in the true knowledge of You and to live according to Your Word.

I ask this all in the name of my Savior, the Lord Jesus Christ.

Date_____

Luke
1:71

Salvation FROM OUR ENEMIES,
AND FROM THE HAND OF ALL WHO HATE US.

Seven

*Your Enemies Are
Already Defeated*

*H*as someone risen up as your enemy because of your relationship with Jesus Christ? It's distressing, isn't it? Sometimes even scary, or at least heavy on your heart. Rest, Beloved. Jesus assured us that if the world hated Him, it will hate us also (John 15:18-25). For now, you are to love those who hate you and pray for them (Matthew 5:43-48). Of all people, your enemies are to be pitied, for they shall ultimately be defeated, destroyed, and punished forever unless they repent and follow your example and receive your Savior.

Therefore, Beloved, don't fear the enemy who threatens your life and your well-being; rather, fear God, who is able to cast both body and soul into hell (Matthew 10:28). Anything God permits your enemies to do is only for His glory and your ultimate good. Enemies drive you to greater dependence upon God as you seek His strength and peace.

I remember reading the account of a dear North Korean pastor and his flock of 27 men, women, and children who lived in underground tunnels to escape the persecution of their government's communist regime. Their hiding place was uncovered when a road was built through the village of Gok San in the 1950s.

The officials brought these Christians before a crowd of 30,000 for a public trial, where they were given the option of denying Christ or dying. Of course, to them, denial was not an option. They had embraced God's horn of salvation. They knew that they were to be faithful unto death. When they refused to deny Christ,

> the head Communist officer ordered four children from the group seized and had them prepared for hanging. After tying ropes around their small necks, the officer again commanded the parents to deny Christ.
>
> Not one of the believers would deny their faith. They told the children, "We will soon see you in heaven." The children died quietly.
>
> The officer called for a steamroller. He forced the Christians to lie on the ground in its path. As its engine revved, they were given one last chance to recant their faith in Jesus. Again they refused.

As the steamroller began to inch forward, the Christians began to sing a song they had often sung together. As their bones and bodies were crushed under the pressure of the massive rollers, their lips uttered the words:

> More love to Thee, O Christ, more love to Thee
> Thee alone I seek, more love to Thee
> Let sorrow do its work, more love to Thee
> Then shall my latest breath whisper Thy praise
> This be the parting cry my heart shall raise;
> More love, O Christ, to Thee.[1]

Although the execution was reported in the North Korean press as an act of suppressing superstition, the testimony is preserved for us to build our faith and to assure us that His offer of peace is for every generation because our God is a covenant-keeping God.

These men, women, and children confessed Christ before men with no fear of what might happen to them (Matthew 10:32). As Zacharias prophesied, God remembers "His holy covenant, the oath which He swore to Abraham our father, to grant us that we, being rescued from the hand of our enemies, might serve Him without fear, in holiness and righteousness all our days" (Luke 1:72-74). Christ has already defeated our earthly oppressors.

Luke tells us that the baby who was named John and circumcised on the eighth day "continued to grow and to become strong in spirit, and he lived in the deserts until the day of his public appearance to Israel" (Luke 1:80). The Prince of Peace would come, and John the Baptist would guide God's people "into the way of peace."

Peace. Be still, Beloved; we already have salvation from our enemies and from all who hate us.

But what if your enemies are not flesh and blood? Perhaps they are the voices within, the memories of days past. Maybe you need salvation from the anguish of a life of failure, of some willful act of disobedience, or of apparent bondage to a nagging craving.

The redemption God has accomplished applies to these torments as well. It includes redemption from all that you were before you came to know Christ. First, remember that the "old you," as Romans 6 teaches, is dead. He was crucified with Christ, buried with Him, and the "new you" has been raised with Christ to walk in newness of life. By an act of God, the past is past. You cannot undo it; you cannot change it. Neither is necessary. God's got it covered! So walk in faith. Put away the dark reasoning of your unregenerate self, the memories of days gone by. Put up your tombstone. Date it with the day of your salvation. You have been crucified with Christ, and the life you now live you are to live by the faith of the Son of God (Galatians 2:20).

Then, if thoughts of what was or what might have been come knocking on the door of your mind, bolt the door. It's your enemy, Satan, prowling about like a roaring lion, seeking to devour you with regrets from your past. Don't let him in, regardless of how hard he pounds on the door of your mind. Grab a cup of tea or coffee and read the Word. It's your security deadbolt.

And what if your enemy is some nagging craving, an addictive behavior? Remember, if you are His, you are already liberated from sin, which includes any addictive dependence that is destroying you. God has raised up a horn of salvation for you. You don't have to yield any part of your body as a slave to anything. Open your Bible: It's right there in Romans 6. If you'll do what God tells you to do in Romans 6:12-14, you'll know victory—temptation by temptation—until finally the warfare subsides.

As I write this I cannot help but think of my radiant friend James. James was a cocaine and crack addict who was delivered the very day he truly repented and called upon the name of the Lord. The sins of his past are covered by the blood of Christ, and he is able to have victory because he does what Romans 6:12-14 says. James knows he's a new creation in

Christ Jesus. He need not hang his head in shame. Neither should you if you have chosen that narrow, straight way that leads to eternal life.

O Father, Father, why do I allow myself to be overcome by people or circumstances, when You tell me right here that You have visited me in Your Son? You have brought me redemption—not only forgiveness of sins but also the promise that my enemies will not ultimately triumph over me. You promise that You will rescue me from the hands of those who hate me. O Father, thank You for Your tender mercy. Thank You for the record of Your words through Zacharias on the day of John's circumcision. Thank You for the salvation You have brought. You have saved me from not only sin's penalty but also sin's power. I thank You that I can yield my body to You as an instrument of righteousness rather than to sin as a slave. Remind me of this, temptation by temptation, regardless of what I face. I thank You that You say in 1 Corinthians 10:13 that You will not allow me to be tempted beyond what I can bear and that You will always provide a way of escape. By Your grace I will believe Your Word and live accordingly.

I thank You also, Father, that You tell me I can serve You without fear, in holiness and righteousness all the days of my life. Help me to keep my eyes on You. Help me to honor You as God by believing and living by every single word in Your Book.

How I look forward to the day when the Sunrise from on high will visit us again as King of kings and Lord of lords! Guide my feet this day into the way of peace. May I neither fight my enemies nor despise them, for unless You have mercy on them they shall perish for ever and ever.

Finally, Father, help me to be like John the Baptist. May I be Jesus' forerunner, telling others about Him, calling them to repent, to have a change of mind and heart that they, too, might have forgiveness of sins and know the power of salvation. As I go about the tasks of daily living today, may I act rather than react in the difficult situations of life. May I live in such a way that the world might see the difference my relationship with Your Son, Jesus Christ, makes, and may those around me be drawn to Him.

I ask this in the name that is above every other name—the name of my Redeemer, my Liberator, Your Son, Jesus Christ. Amen.

Luke 2:1-6

Now in those days a decree went out from Caesar Augustus, that a census be taken of all the inhabited earth. This was the first census taken while Quirinius was governor of Syria. And everyone was on his way to register for the census, each to his own city. Joseph also went up from Galilee, from the city of Nazareth, to Judea, to the City of David which is called Bethlehem, because he was of the house and family of David, in order to register along with Mary, who was engaged to him, and was with child. While they were there, the days were completed for her to give birth.

Eight

His Promises Are Always on Schedule

Do you sometimes panic, wondering where God is as the nations and rebel governments plot and plan and make war, forming coalitions in rebellion against God and bringing untold grief to multitudes?

Rest, dear child of God. God has not left His throne. What God has purposed will not be thwarted. His promises are all on schedule, under His timing, just as they were when the time came for the birth of Messiah, the promised One of God, almost two thousand years ago.

About nine months had passed since the angel Gabriel visited Mary. Although her promised Son was probably due any day, Mary went with Joseph to Bethlehem, the city of David, for the census. The journey of 70 to 80 miles was a difficult trip, but Joseph could not avoid it. No one in his right mind would disobey a decree from the ruler who took to himself the title Caesar "Augustus"—the exalted one.

The census, as far as we know, did not require a wife to accompany her husband. Even if it did, Joseph and Mary had not yet consummated their marriage, for Joseph "kept her a virgin until she gave birth to a Son" (Matthew 1:25).

What prompted Mary to go with Joseph? Was it because she could not bear to be apart from her betrothed at the birth of her son, and she feared Joseph might not return in time? Or was it because of the possible shame and reproach she might bear if Joseph left her alone in Nazareth?

From man's perspective, we don't know, but from God's, we do.

The Son of God, of the womb of Mary, had to be born in the city of David, Bethlehem Ephrathah. Bethlehem Ephrathah—the city where Boaz took the Gentile Ruth as a bride. To Ruth was born Obed, the father of Jesse, the father of the shepherd boy David (Ruth 4:17-22). Bethlehem Ephrathah—the city where David was anointed by the prophet Samuel as the next king of Israel (1 Samuel 16:1-4).

Every 14 years, Rome took a census for military and tax purposes. In a Jewish census, every family was kept distinct; therefore, every Jewish male was required to return to the city of his fathers and there record his name, occupation, property, and family.[2] Four years prior to this, Rome had moved to tax the Jewish people, but a loud protest from the land of Israel delayed the census, and no Jew was conscripted into the army of Rome![3] Of all the nations Rome ever ruled, none was more rebellious or more vocal than Israel. That's why a census hadn't been taken before.

However, there was no protest this time. The fullness of time had come for God's Son to be born of a woman, born under the Law (Galatians 4:4). Let all proceed as planned! This was a census decreed by God—the first census, taken by Quirinius, who was governor of Syria not once but twice.

The One in Mary's womb could not be born in Nazareth, although he would be called a Nazarene. Micah prophesied:

> But as for you, Bethlehem Ephrathah,
> Too little to be among the clans of Judah,
> From you One will go forth for Me to be ruler in
>   Israel.
> His goings forth are from long ago,
> From the days of eternity (Micah 5:2).

From the days of eternity, God had planned not only the birth of His Son but also His death; He would be crucified on the very day the Israelites would be slaying their Passover lambs. The One in Mary's womb was the Lamb slain before the foundation of the world for the redemption of man.

The One born of Mary would come—*must* come—from the lineage of Judah through the family of David.

Jacob's dying prophecy to his son Judah was about to be fulfilled. Shiloh, Messiah, the One to whom the throne of

David belongs, was about to be born. The scepter would not depart from Judah, Jacob had promised, nor the ruler's staff from between his feet, until Shiloh came, and to him would be the obedience of the people (Genesis 49:10).

The fulfillment of God's covenant promise to David was now underway. God would begin to build His kingdom on earth, and we would be part of His house (Hebrews 3:1-6).

> When your days are complete and you lie down with your fathers, I will raise up your descendant after you, who will come forth from you, and I will establish his kingdom. He shall build a house for My name, and I will establish the throne of his kingdom forever (2 Samuel 7:12-13).

The decree of an idolatrous empire, the decree that required the whole known world to be taxed, was in God's timing, proving to all that Jesus was of the tribe of Judah, the family of David. The Pharisees knew the prophecy: Christ, Messiah, had to come from the lineage of David; He had to be a son of David.

> Now while the Pharisees were gathered together, Jesus asked them a question: "What do you think about the Christ, whose son is He?"

> They said to Him, "The son of David" (Matthew 22:41-42).

When Jesus healed the blind man, the multitudes asked, "This man cannot be the Son of David, can he?" (Matthew 12:23). They, too, were looking for Messiah and knew that Messiah had to be the Son of David.

Even a Canaanite woman would beg for His help and identify Him as the Son of David when she cried out, "Have mercy on me, Lord, Son of David; my daughter is cruelly demon-possessed" (Matthew 15:22).

Two blind men sitting by the road, hearing that Jesus was passing by, would also cry out, saying "Lord, have mercy on us, Son of David!" (Matthew 20:30).

And on that epochal day prophesied by Zechariah, when Jesus rode into Jerusalem on a donkey, the multitudes clearly identified Him as their King, crying out of one accord, "Hosanna to the Son of David; BLESSED IS HE WHO COMES IN THE NAME OF THE LORD; Hosanna in the highest!" (Matthew 21:9).

Every Jew could trace his own genealogy. "All Israel was enrolled by genealogies" (1 Chronicles 9:1). Records were kept in cities and were public property until Jerusalem's fall (Nehemiah 7:5-6; Ezra 2). The records were used to prove one's lineage.

Even the lineage of Jesus the Nazarene.

However, if Jesus had been born after A.D. 70, when Titus the Roman general razed Jerusalem and the temple and destroyed the public records, Jesus could not have proven His Davidic line. So God used the decree of a Roman ruler, Caesar Augustus, sometime between 6 B.C. and 4 B.C., to establish the genealogy of His Son.

The fullness of time had come. Over 333 prophecies were about to be fulfilled over the next 33 years. His genealogy was one of the ways that Jesus would be identified as the Christ, *ha Mashiyach.*

For if He's *not* the Christ—

the seed of the woman promised in Genesis 3:15,

the seed promised by covenant to Abraham through his son Isaac,

and from Isaac to Jacob, whose name was changed to Israel,

then through Jacob to his son Judah,

and from Judah to David,

and through a virgin of the house of David,

who will be with child and bear a son,

whose name shall be Immanuel, "God with us,"—

—then, Beloved, you and I are lost because of *our* genealogy. If Jesus is not the Christ, there is no one outside the lineage of Adam to redeem us.

And what of your genealogy and mine? If the records were kept on earth as they are in heaven, you could trace your lineage all the way back to Noah and one of his sons, Shem, Ham, or Japheth,

    and right back to Adam,

        the one man through whom came sin and death by sin.

And there you and I would stand, Beloved, condemned with all mankind for all time because "the wages of sin is death" (Romans 6:23) and "the soul who sins will die" (Ezekiel 18:4). The death sin brings is not annihilation. Rather, it is hell in all its torment, eternity spent in the lake of fire. It's the second death, where the worm never dies and the blaze is not quenched (Mark 9:48)!

Jesus' genealogy, however, takes a hiatus from all mankind. Not because of His mother, for He was born of woman even as you and I are, but because of His Father, for Jesus' Father is God Almighty.

Jesus' mother, Mary, makes Jesus the Son of Man.

Jesus' Father, God, makes Him the Son of God.

Jesus, then, God's only begotten Son, is God incarnate, God in the flesh, the only One born without sin so He could be made sin for you and die in your place!

Little did the government of Rome realize how they were serving the government of heaven.

In this, Beloved, you can rest assured that what God has promised will never fail to come to pass. Although you see the nations in conflict, and hear of wars and rumors of war, and watch militant Islam raise its fist to the West, you can know that although these nations and governments neither know God nor honor His Son as God, they will serve His purpose until He is through with them. The nations are aligning for the final battle. The world will fall under the dominion of ten of them. Then God's Son shall come again, this time for judgment, and every knee will bow and every tongue will confess that Jesus is Lord, to the glory of the Father (Philippians 2:9-11).

"The Lord has established His throne in the heavens, and His sovereignty rules over all" (Psalm 103:19). The Lord of hosts has made His plans, and who can frustrate them (Isaiah 14:24,27)?

O Father, Almighty God, El Elyon—the Most High, You are in Your holy temple, and we bow before You in silence. We worship You and wonder:

> *Why are the nations in an uproar,*
> *And the peoples devising a vain thing?*

> *The kings of the earth take their stand*
> *And the rulers take counsel together*
> *Against the* LORD *and against His Anointed, saying,*
> *"Let us tear their fetters apart*
> *And cast away their cords from us!" (Psalm 2:1-3).*

You sit in the heavens and laugh. You scoff at them. You have installed Your King upon Zion, Your holy mountain. You have said to our Savior, "You are My Son, today I have begotten You. Ask of Me, and I will surely give the nations as Your inheritance, and the very ends of the earth as Your possession."

You will break them with a rod of iron, You will shatter them like earthenware.

Your wrath will soon be kindled.

Bless me, Lord, as I await and prepare for that day, as I take refuge in Your Christ (Psalm 2:4-12). Protect me as I wait patiently for the Son of God, the Son of Man born in the City of David, the One destined to establish Your kingdom on earth and to rule from Jerusalem, Your earthly Zion in the land of Israel (Daniel 7:13-14,27).

John 1:1-13

In the beginning was the Word, and the Word was with God, and the Word was God. He was in the beginning with God. All things came into being through Him, and apart from Him nothing came into being that has come into being. In Him was life, and the life was the Light of men. The Light shines in the darkness, and the darkness did not comprehend it.

There came a man sent from God, whose name was John. He came as a witness, to testify about the Light, so that all might believe through him. He was not the Light, but he came to testify about the Light.

There was the true Light which, coming into the world, enlightens every man. He was in the world, and the world was made through Him, and the world did not know Him. He came to His own, and those who were His own did not receive Him. But as many as received Him, to them He gave the right to become children of God, even to those who believe in His name, who were born, not of blood nor of the will of the flesh, nor of the will of man, but of God.

Nine

*He Was There
All the Time*

*H*ave you ever asked, "God, where were You when _____? Why didn't You _____?"

What experiences fill your first blank? Probably events you wish God would have stopped, stepped into, or changed to make things different, better for you. *This* would have had a more favorable outcome. *That* wouldn't have been destroyed. *They* would have—what?

How can we know what this or that or they would have been? Are we not mere mortals? We can't know, can we? We can only suppose.

But God knows because He is God. Yet He doesn't tell us why He does what He does. He doesn't explain. He doesn't have to because He is God. All we have to do is trust Him.

I believe that scriptures such as John 1:1-2 help us to trust. I believe God wants us to know that Jesus has been a part of history, a part of forever, *forever.* He has been in existence since the beginning of time; in fact, before the beginning of time.

Jesus has always been standing in the wings of human history. Offstage. Behind the curtains of time. Unseen. Unrecognized.

That is, until He became man.

From the dawning of the ages He was there, eternal. Fully God. Equal with the Father.

Thus, when the Spirit of God moved the apostle John to take up his quill and author a fourth and final Gospel—years after Matthew, Mark, and Luke had penned their accounts—God would make sure we understood that Jesus was not a newcomer on the stage of history. Rather, He who had been one with the Father from all of eternity had simply been revealed in the fullness of time as God in the flesh, the incarnate Deity.

Here, in this mystery of our Lord's timelessness, is where you can find peace with your past.

If you long for a mental and emotional reconciliation with your past—if you long to let it go and welcome a future unencumbered by the "what ifs," the "might have beens," and the "if onlys"—you must understand Jesus was there, through all your experiences, all the time. God didn't move until He wanted to move. An eternal purpose and timing prevails in all He does. In other words, Jesus knew; Jesus saw, even if you didn't see Him move. Maybe He didn't stop you. Maybe He didn't rescue you. Maybe He didn't intervene on your behalf. *But He was there.*

When we consciously, rationally let go of our past, with all its embarrassing foibles and excruciating pain, and move into the future, we find peace in the One who has made the beauty of our future certain. With Christ in our history, our future is as rich and hope-filled as the power and promises of God. This, Beloved, is what brings the "peace on earth" we sing about at Christmas when we celebrate His birth.

Such peace seems an empty promise in the light of the world's turmoil until you turn to the text in Luke 2:14 that inspired the hymn writer: "Glory to God in the highest, and on earth peace among men with whom He is pleased." Clearly, God reserves His peace for those with whom He is pleased.

One may ask with indignation or fright, "And who, pray tell, are those?" Hebrews 11:6 answers the question: God is pleased with those who take Him at His Word, with those who believe Him. For without faith, neither you nor I nor anyone else will ever please God. Peace, Beloved, is the satisfying, soul-sustaining harvest of faith.

So what does this passage in the Gospel of John reveal that can quench your torment? How can it answer your questions about where God was in your time of need and why He didn't act as you thought He should?

Let's go back to those opening verses: "In the beginning was the Word, and the Word was with God, and the Word was God. He was in the beginning with God. All things came into being through Him, and apart from Him nothing came into being that has come into being. In Him was life…."

Jesus—the Word—was there all the time, from eternity past. He has always been. He will always be. He is the author of our lives. And in Him—in Him alone—we find life.

Not long ago I stood in the largest women's prison in the world. I was in fact in "the prison within the prison," an inner facility where already-incarcerated women are locked up because they have allegedly broken the prison's rules. Desperation, defeat, and a seething anger hung in the air. Despair covered their faces like sweat from the heavy humidity of a sweltering summer day. Women of all ages and descriptions were locked behind huge solid metal doors painted a dirty brown maroon. A "doggy door" at the bottom permitted guards to slide things in and out of the cell. Whenever a woman left the cell, she was led in chains by two guards wearing flack jackets and face shields.

I was overwhelmed by the awesome privilege of being invited into a part of the prison where few outsiders ever went. I was excited by the prospect of proclaiming the pure, unadulterated, life-giving truth of the Word of God while armed guards worked around me, standing at my back.

I began, "It is such an honor to be able to come here and to be with you."

My voice trembled with emotion. It was indeed an honor, a great privilege ordained by Almighty God. The opportunity came about because of the faithfulness and integrity of Mary Alice, a woman who visited the prison weekly to teach the women how to study their Bibles precept upon precept. The effectiveness of her witness granted me an open door, and I decided to walk through it because I knew Mary Alice would continue her faithful work after I was gone. She would disciple these women. She would give them both the milk and the meat of God's Word so essential to their growth. She would teach them how to study God's Word inductively so they could know truth for themselves.

I knew I had a message that could transform the lives of these women and set them free even if they never left that prison. It was a message of hope and life, a message that would shatter the shackles of their past, even as it had shattered mine. It was a message of *the One:*

- The One who brought each one of those women into existence, even though He knew they would sin and rebel against His Father and against His commandments, even though He knew their ungodly choices would blaspheme His name and His character.

- The One who was born for the sole purpose of "taking the rap" for them, dying in their place, attaining forgiveness for their sins so that they wouldn't be condemned before God's holy tribunal.

- The One who, although He had been a part of history since the beginning, willingly "became flesh, and dwelt among us" so that we could behold His glory, the glory "of the only begotten from the Father, full of grace and truth" (John 1:14).

- The Son of God, the lover of their souls.

Pause with me for a moment, my friend, and think about it:

- This is the Word, the One who was in the beginning with God, the One who was God but *became flesh.* As a human creature He was tempted in every way that these women have ever been tempted—in every way that you and I have been tempted—and yet never yielded.

- This is the One able to sympathize with our weakness and who, even though He was the Son of God, learned obedience as He suffered. He, too, cried, wept, and called on God to rescue Him.

- This is the One who became flesh and blood for the sole purpose of dying for us! He knew that through death He would strip the devil of his power and deliver us from Satan's bonds.

- This is the One who will not leave us as orphans.

- This is the One who has sent us the Spirit of God, the third member of the Godhead, to indwell us and through His power enable everyone—these women, you, me—to obey God's commandments and walk in a way that is pleasing to our Father, God Almighty (John 14:16-18)!

- This is the One who was there all the time; even so, He chose the fullness of God's time to reveal Himself *to* us and *in* us so that we all might become children of the living God, new creatures in Christ Jesus who have an inheritance in heaven, an imperishable, undefiled inheritance reserved just for us (1 Peter 1:4).

I taught these precious women scripture after scripture for about an hour and a half. As I spoke, more and more women turned on their cell lights. They peered through the narrow perpendicular windows bordering the maroon iron doors that protected others from them. They made notes on paper held up against the windows, recording the address of each biblical truth. From time to time, I would watch as a cloth or a sleeve cleared away the fog created by their tears and heavy breathing. It seemed for many of us—prisoner and teacher—that we couldn't get close enough to one another.

Finally I invited them to believe, to receive Christ and with Him the promise that God has granted them everything that pertains to life and godliness through the true knowledge of Jesus, who had just called them by His glory and excellence. With all confidence I could assure them that the God of all hope would supernaturally make them partakers of the divine nature, enabling them to escape the corruption that is in the world by lust (2 Peter 1:2-4). I could not promise them release from prison, but I could assure them that whether in prison or out they could be free from slavery to sin. Whether shackled in chains every time they left "the prison within the prison," never again would they be bound by sin. Those who believed in Jesus Christ and received Him as their God and Savior would be united to Jesus through His death, burial, and resurrection. In their very act of faith, they would die to their own life and be raised with Christ to walk in newness of life (Romans 6:4).

The One who had been there all the time had been revealed to them now because it pleased God. The Christ had been born, and they could be born again into His forever family.[4]

"I can't see all your faces because some of you are too far away," I explained, "but, dear ones, if you have truly repented and believed and received Jesus Christ as your God and Savior, then would you put your hand on the window until I move with my eyes from window to window, acknowledging that I have seen your confession of faith?"

Hand after hand graced the windows, meeting the hand of the extravagant, lavish grace of God in the person of Jesus, "the only begotten from the Father, full of grace and truth."

And what happened for these women at that moment in eternity? The same that has happened for everyone at the moment of confessing faith in the Word made flesh. John explains: "For of His fullness we have all received, and grace upon grace. For the Law was given through Moses; grace and truth were realized through Jesus Christ" (John 1:16-17).

At last, in God's time, in this place, those dear women recognized the One who had been there all the time, waiting behind the curtain of time for the moment when they would invite Him to step onto the stage of their lives, when He could finally take the leading role in the drama of their redemption.

These women's old nature—all that they were before they received Christ—died that day (Romans 6:6). They were brand new! Now they needed to know how to live accordingly, and they could because the Spirit of God indwelt them (Romans 8:1-17). Also, God had ordained that His servant

Mary Alice would continue to teach them how to live by every word that came from His mouth as recorded in the Word of God. The studies from Precept Ministries International would also assist them as they grew into their full stature as women of God.

We have been redeemed not only from sin's penalty but from sin's power, and someday we will also be free of sin's presence. Truly, the regrets of the past can have no power over a child of God. For unto us a Child has been born, a Son has been given, and the government of our lives now rests on His shoulders (Isaiah 9:6).

O Father, Almighty God, I am so grateful that You were pleased to reveal Your Son in me at just the right time! I stand in awe at the faith of these imprisoned women and am reminded that Your grace is altogether sufficient, that Your power is perfected in weakness, and that there is far more to eternal life than this life. This is but the beginning.

O Father, forgive me when I waste my time and my energy rummaging through my past. What futility! It can never be changed. It is done. Over. May I instead remember that You were there all the time—the eternal

Father, Son, and Holy Spirit. You could have saved me sooner than You did—but You didn't; therefore I will look forward to the fulfillment of Your purpose and plan for me. You saved me when You were pleased to, and because You are the Redeemer, I trust You will use even my past for Your purposes and for Your glory.

The birth of Your Son marked the inauguration of the era of the New Covenant. My birth in Him marked the inauguration of Your New Covenant of grace in my life. May I walk in the fullness of this era, remembering "I have been crucified with Christ; and it is no longer I who live, but Christ lives in me; and the life which I now live in the flesh I live by faith in the Son of God, who loved me and gave Himself up for me" (Galatians 2:20).

Thank You, Lord, that Your divine power has granted me everything that pertains to life and godliness through the true knowledge of Him who called me by His own glory and excellence (2 Peter 1:3). Now may I discipline myself to pursue that knowledge, growing more and more in my understanding of You, of Your Son, of the blessed indwelling Holy Spirit, and of course, Your precepts for life.

I ask this in the name of the One who has been there all the time, Immanuel.

Luke
2:7

And she gave birth to her firstborn son; and she wrapped him in cloths.

Ten

Do You Know What You Have?

As Mary drew her firstborn to her breast, enveloping him with love, did she realize she was cradling eternity in her arms? Did she know she held the Word, as God tells us in the Gospel of John, who existed before the beginning of time? The Word who was with God? Who was God? The Alpha and the Omega? Creator of all?

Did she know the life she had birthed was the source of all life? The Light of life who enlightens every man, making him aware that there is a God outside himself?

Did she know this One alone could rescue mankind from the kingdom of darkness?

Did Mary realize she held the Mediator of the New Covenant promised by God centuries earlier through the prophet Jeremiah? The One who would bring grace upon grace to all mankind? The One who would restore God's favor toward us—unearned and undeserved, but available to all?

And with that grace would come truth.

Mary held Truth—unadulterated Truth!—in her arms. Our only glimpse of perfection in humanity.

The One nestled against her breasts was the *only* begotten Son of God, the One who would explain the Father to all who would listen. He would speak the Father's words and demonstrate the Father's works so that by listening to Him, by watching Him, we would hear and see the unseen Father.

The One who laid against Mary's bosom had rested in God's bosom from eternity past. The eyes she gazed into so adoringly belonged to the very Lamb of God, the One who would take away the sins of the world—including hers. He would baptize every single believer in the Holy Spirit, sealing them until the day of their physical redemption, guaranteeing them eternal life.

The child Mary would raise and instruct in the fear and admonition of the Lord was Messiah, the Christ, the true Rabbi, the teacher from God, the fulfillment of the Law and the Prophets.

The One Mary held was the Son of God, the King of Israel.

Is it any wonder Mark Lowry's song "Mary, Did You Know?" so captivated our hearts as we recalled in awe the birth of Mary's baby boy?

Mary may not have known all this when she gave birth to Jesus. Although she held the Word of God made flesh, in all probability she didn't have her own copy of the Scriptures. She only knew what was read to her in the synagogue, Sabbath after Sabbath. The rabbis would discuss the Word, but it was not for the women to study and debate. They were to sit in the women's section and be quiet.

What a juxtaposition we experience today! Though none of us has seen the Word who became flesh, we have the written Word of God, the revelation of Jesus Christ, which tells us all about the Savior of the world.

But where is it? What prominence does God's Word have in your life? Is it like a child you cherish and hold close or an abandoned baby?

Beloved, do you know whom you have and what you have when you have Jesus? God wants you to know. He wants you to understand how rich you are because you have Jesus. And He wants you to order your life accordingly.

As God tells us in the first chapter of Hebrews, Jesus is the firstborn, whom He brought into the world, the Son whom He has begotten, the One whom He will father, the One whose throne is forever and ever. He is the One who laid the foundations of the earth, who created the heavens and all the works of His hands. He is the One who will remain, whose years will never come to an end.

Jesus is God, the great I AM. By embracing this truth in a simple but profound act of faith, you gain eternal life.

How incredible! How awesome! When you receive Jesus, the One who for the most part is rejected by His own people, the Jews, you gain the right and the privilege, even if you are a Gentile, of becoming a child of God Almighty! Although you once had no hope, although you were once excluded from the covenants of God's promises, you can become the dwelling place of God!

Light shines in the darkness, and the darkness disappears. You have the Light of life! You know who you are! Why you were born! Why you are living! Where you are going! And you know you will live for ever and ever and ever in the glorious presence of God the Father, God the Son, and God the Holy Spirit. Nothing, *nothing*, will ever separate you from the love of God, which is in Christ Jesus, your Lord (Romans 8:38-39).

As a mother draws her child to her breast and muses about his future, may I urge you, Beloved, to draw the Word of God close to your heart and meditate on all that is yours for now and eternity because of the Son born to Mary.

O Father, as Mary cradled the Word in her arms, may I cradle Your Word, the Bible, in mine. May it become more precious to me than the temporal trinkets and treasures of this life. More treasured than the words

of man. More dear than the opinions, reports, news, and entertainment that blare on and on day in and day out.

May I seek quiet places of refuge where I can be alone with You and Your Son through Your Word; where I can, by Your Spirit, seek out truth. May I find a place where the din of the world is silenced and I can hear You clearly as I read and wait for You to quicken my heart with truth.

You say Your Word is truth—that which sanctifies me, sets me apart, makes me holy, consecrates me to You. You tell me it will wash my soul, cleanse my conscience, and give me the sense of peace that comes only when I know all is right between You and me.

May I learn to live in the sweetness of Your presence and the fullness of joy that comes from knowing You and knowing all is right between You and me. Fill my heart with lullabies of love to Your Son, my Savior and my God.

I pray this in the name of Your only begotten Son. Amen.

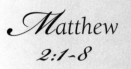

Matthew
2:1-8

Now after Jesus was born in Bethlehem of Judea in the days of Herod the king, magi from the east arrived in Jerusalem, saying, "Where is He who has been born King of the Jews? For we saw His star in the east and have come to worship Him." When Herod the king heard it, he was troubled, and all Jerusalem with him. Gathering together all the chief priests and scribes of the people, he inquired of them where the Messiah was to be born. They said to him, "In Bethlehem of Judea; for this is what has been written by the prophet:

    'AND YOU, BETHLEHEM, LAND OF JUDAH,

    ARE BY NO MEANS LEAST AMONG THE LEADERS OF JUDAH;

    FOR OUT OF YOU SHALL COME FORTH A RULER

    WHO WILL SHEPHERD MY PEOPLE ISRAEL.' "

Then Herod secretly called the magi and determined from them the exact time the star appeared. And he sent them to Bethlehem and said, "Go and search carefully for the Child; and when you have found Him, report to me, so that I too may come and worship Him."

Eleven

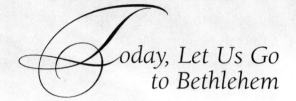

oday, Let Us Go to Bethlehem

*C*hristmas. It's the most anticipated, celebrated, advertised holiday of the year. To some, the holiday is purely secular, focused on giving and receiving, long in coming and short in true celebration, leaving little in its wake but exhaustion, debt, and disappointment. Yet to others, like you and me, Christmas is one of the most precious times of year, for Christmas reminds us that "today in the city of David there has been born *for you* a Savior, who is Christ the Lord" (Luke 2:11).

But is it possible that Christmas could be more than this, more than one special day centered on Jesus? There must be more to this annual event than going back to life as usual after the presents are opened, dinner is eaten, family and friends have gone home, and the house is put back in order. There must be more joy on December 26 than can be found in noting that we have 364 shopping days until next year!

Is our celebration of Christ's birth supposed to be that way, just a daylong or seasonal celebration?

No, Beloved. I say this because the events that occurred not too long after the birth of Jesus point to something greater. If we open our eyes and ears to the lessons in these events, what we discover could trigger a spiritual awakening in your life and mine in the days and months ahead.

Let's look at what Matthew tells us that the other gospels don't about this time surrounding Christ's birth. Although traditionally we place the wise men next to the shepherds in our manger scenes, Matthew tells us that it was some time *after* Jesus was born in Bethlehem that the magi arrived in Jerusalem. These men from the East had seen His star and were looking for the One who had been born King of the Jews. Matthew leaves us no doubt as to the reason for their journey: They had come to worship Him.

When Herod heard of the magi and the commotion their visit stirred in Jerusalem, he secretly summoned these men. Why? Herod, who served as king of the Jews under the authority of Rome, said that he, too, wanted to come and worship Him.

But Herod lied.

Herod did not want to worship the Christ; he wanted to destroy Him.

How foolish Herod was to think that he could fight against God! How arrogant to think that an earthly king could counteract a decree from the throne of the Sovereign Ruler of all the universe! This, after all, was the birth decreed before the foundation of the world.

Listen to what Matthew tells us:

> After hearing the king, they went their way; and the star, which they had seen in the east, went on before them until it came and stood over the place where the Child was. When they saw the star, they rejoiced exceedingly with great joy. After coming into the house they saw the Child with Mary His mother; and they fell to the ground and worshiped Him. Then, opening their treasures, they presented to Him gifts of gold, frankincense, and myrrh. And having been warned by God in a dream not to return to Herod, the magi left for their own country by another way.
>
> Now when they had gone, behold, an angel of the Lord appeared to Joseph in a dream and said, "Get up! Take the Child and His mother and flee to Egypt, and remain there until I tell you; for Herod is going to search for the Child to destroy Him...."
>
> But when Herod died... (Matthew 2:9-13,19).

What a profound lesson there is for us in this second chapter of Matthew.

When the magi and the king wanted to find the Christ, the chief priests and the scribes were able to tell them where He was. He was not in Jerusalem, the earthly Zion, but in Bethlehem of Judea. As with all the other prophecies concerning Messiah, the city of His birth had been chiseled forever into the granite of God's Word. It was the prophet Micah who distinguished Bethlehem Ephrathah, the city of David in the land of Judah, from the other Bethlehems of Israel.

Does it amaze you that Herod did not want to accompany the magi to see for himself this One who had been born? It did me, until I considered the reminder in Ecclesiastes that there is nothing new under the sun. Some people simply don't want to know truth unless they can see something in it for them. If this Child the magi sought was really the King of the Jews, then He was nothing more than a threat to Herod, who considered *himself* the king of the Jews. This Christ was a menace, not a hope!

So the magi made their way without Herod to the small city of Bethlehem south of Jerusalem. Once they found Him, they could not contain their joy! Their knees crumbled in awe. Their faces were on the ground. And they did what they had come to do: They worshiped Him and spread their treasures before Him. This Child was far more than a king, for the

One with Mary was the only begotten Son of God, the Son of Man, the Lamb of God slain before the foundation of the world, the King of kings!

Herod missed Christmas! It passed him by because in his mind, life was all about him. He was a jealous man, jealous of his own glory.

Herod ignored the Word of God and the witness of men, both of which pointed to the arrival of Messiah, God made man. In order to preserve his own desires, Herod had to get around truth; he had to silence it. So he plotted. He would speak to the magi secretly. He would lie, claiming that he, too, wanted to worship the Christ. He would develop a scheme to destroy the One who laid claim to his title, king of the Jews. Although old and sick and trying to hold death at bay, he would do anything necessary to squelch his usurpers. He would die for his earthly throne rather than embrace Eternal Life, who was just a short journey away.

How incredibly sad. Herod's cup of iniquity overflowed with the blood of all who threatened him in any way, not only his enemies. Family members, friends, politicians, and even Miriam, the wife he adored, were killed for nothing more than the security of his own benefice. History recorded his sins, and so did God. Hell would enlarge its borders to receive him.

And yet, for all his iniquity, Herod could have gone to Bethlehem. He could have seen the Christ, the One born King of the Jews. He could have worshiped Him, prostrated himself before the Lamb of God who would take away his sins. He, too, could have known exceedingly great joy, joy that had the power to override, cover, and pardon the horrific past that now tormented him.

But no. The Savior of the world had been born, and Herod refused to worship Him. Instead, he added to his sins the most notorious of his crimes—the slaughter of all the male children two years and younger who lived in Bethlehem's environs (Matthew 2:16-18).

And what do we read in the final commentary on Herod in the book of Matthew? "But when Herod died...."

Herod died. Jesus lived.

And He lives today. Jesus is seated at the right hand of the throne of God, where He continuously makes intercession for us—for you, Beloved—by name. Soon He will rise from His Father's throne, mount His white horse, and return to earth to reign not only as King of the Jews, but as King of kings and Lord of lords. And then, after His reign of a thousand years, death and Hades will give up their dead. The books will be opened, and the small and the great whose names are not written in the book of life—even Herod—will be consigned to the lake of fire for all eternity.

It is one thing to prepare for Christmas, my friend, to remember and celebrate Christ's first appearance on earth in the flesh. Let us also prepare daily for His second return. Let us prostrate ourselves before Him in total submission, day in and day out, and not just at Christmas. Let us give Him the gift of our complete adoration, laying every treasure we possess at His feet.

O Beloved, this could be a most significant act of worship in your life, a habit that generates spiritual renewal, an experience of unshakable joy and multiplied peace given to those who willingly honor Him as He should be honored—as God.

I want to mine more practical lessons from this passage in Matthew; however, before I do, let's go to our God in prayer.

O Father, I do not want to mimic the world in any way when it comes to what Christmas is all about. As I prepare mentally, emotionally, and spiritually to celebrate Your unspeakable gift in Jesus Christ, show me how to make the holiday all about You and the greatness of Your love all year long. Show me how to make it all about Jesus and His humility in clothing Himself with humanity. Show me how to make it all about being filled with Your Spirit so that I will not grieve Him but instead will live in the fullness of all that is mine through the gift of Your Son.

May I view each day as a day to worship You, to adore You, to honor You before others by the way I live, and to speak without shame about Your Son to others so that they might not miss the gift of life, which is found only in receiving the gift of Your Son. Show me ways to share with others the true meaning of Christmas every day of the year.

I bow before You and ask this in the name of Your Son, the Christ, the Ruler of Your people. I thank You for what You are going to do because I know that I ask according to Your Word. Amen.

Matthew 2:9-12

After hearing the king, they went their way; and the star, which they had seen in the east, went on before them until it came and stood over the place where the Child was. When they saw the star, they rejoiced exceedingly with great joy. After coming into the house they saw the Child with Mary His mother; and they fell to the ground and worshiped Him. Then, opening their treasures, they presented to Him gifts of gold, frankincense, and myrrh. And having been warned by God in a dream not to return to Herod, the magi left for their own country by another way.

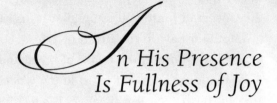

n His Presence Is Fullness of Joy

*W*hen you think of worshiping God, what comes to your mind? So often we think of singing choruses, raising our hands in praise, and being lost in the emotion of adoration. Singing and making melody in our hears to the Lord is indeed one aspect of worship, but there is more. Much more.

The Word of God speaks of a reasonable service of worship, which is "to present your bodies a living and holy sacrifice, acceptable to God" (Romans 12:1). This service of sacrifice refers to acts compelled by who He is and what He asks of us, namely, total submission of our hearts, minds, and bodies to Him. It is this aspect of worship revealed in Matthew 2 that I want us to examine now. Let's see what lessons we can learn that will enrich our daily celebration of Christ's birth as we cherish the greatness of God's gift.

I want us to begin by looking at the significance of Bethlehem as Messiah's birthplace. Biblical names are often rich with meaning of great import; this city chosen by God is no exception. Bethlehem means "the house of bread." Doesn't that make your mind go crazy with delight? If you have read the Gospel of John, you know that Jesus says He is the Bread of Life! Our Savior, the Bread of Life, who came down from heaven, was born in the house of bread and laid in a manger!

Why does God want us to know where His Son was laid after his birth? Because a manger is a feeding trough! What an awesome picture, a Rembrandt of the finest detail. From Abraham, Isaac, Jacob, Judah, and David would come the Bread of Life, sent down from heaven to give spiritual nourishment to the world.

"Come and dine," the Master calls, "for he who eats My flesh and drinks My blood has eternal life, and I will raise him up on the last day" (see John 6:54). The word picture could not be more clear: On the day of Christ's birth, God offered to all mankind the sustaining gift of life and set Him in a manger in the house of bread.

Herod dined sumptuously in this life, yet he perished because he refused the Bread of Life. He said he wanted to worship the Christ, but he didn't mean it.

So what do bread and feeding troughs have to do with worship? Simply this: Worship begins by *receiving and partaking* of the One whom God has provided for eternal life. It continues by *feasting* on Him. We worship God by honoring

His Word, by giving it priority in our lives, even as Jesus did. God said it and Jesus quoted Him: "MAN SHALL NOT LIVE ON BREAD ALONE, BUT ON EVERY WORD THAT PROCEEDS OUT OF THE MOUTH OF GOD" (Matthew 4:4).

O Beloved, if there is a hunger in your life, a craving you cannot seem to fill, or a temptation you feel too weak to overcome, could it be that you are not getting enough of the Bread of Life? Could it be that you are not worshiping Him as you should?

If you want a spiritual awakening in your life,
 a deeper sense of intimacy,
  an exceedingly great joy that cannot be diminished
  by any circumstance,
   then you must feast on Him.

You must meet with your God consistently and faithfully, not because you are commanded to but because you need to. He is your very life and sanity.

Women who recently attended Precept Ministries International's annual women's conferences told me repeatedly that one of their greatest personal frustrations was maintaining a consistent time with their Lord. The pressures and demands on women in our culture today could not be more wearying, yet nothing is more essential to our survival than this sacred time. Men who attended our annual men's conference shared the same frustration. Our greatest need is for time to be still, to have leisure with God, to think through His precepts of life, to do the one thing that is needful—to sit at His feet and learn of Him (Luke 10:38-42). When we have time like this with Him, we have all we need to keep life in perspective.

Even Jesus, the Son of God, had to have this time with His Father. Mark tells us in his Gospel that "in the early morning, while it was still dark, Jesus got up, left the house, and went away to a secluded place, and was praying there" (Mark 1:35).

When Jesus' disciples found Him in that lonely place and told Him that everyone was looking for Him, He said, "Let us go somewhere else to the towns nearby, so that I may preach there also; for that is what I came out for" (verse 38).

Jesus, the Son of Man, began His day by "gathering God's manna in the morning." Because Jesus had been with His Father, He knew that what the people wanted was not what God wanted. He had His direction from God, not from man.

Can you imagine, Beloved, what pressure would be lifted from us if we sat at His feet in His Word day by day, discerning the will of God?

It's interesting, isn't it, that men from the East seeking the King of the Jews awakened the Jews to the fact that their Messiah had finally been born in Bethlehem, just as the Scriptures said. When Herod inquired, the scribes and Pharisees let him know that from Bethlehem would come a

Ruler to shepherd His people. It's in this prophecy, I believe, that we find a second insight into a life of deeper worship. We are not only to feast on Him but also to be led by Him. Jesus is the Ruler and the Shepherd of His people.

Who is your ruler and shepherd, my friend? Who orders your life? Who directs your steps? Who gives you reason to go where you go and do what you do? Who gives you wisdom to say no to some things and yes to others?

I hope your answer is Jesus. He alone can prevent you from turning your own way and, in the process, going astray. Submit to Him. Follow His leadership above the voice of all men, and you will be blessed by God among men.

Finally, do you realize that the more you worship Him, the more you will want to give Him? Your desires will be overtaken by the desire to further God's kingdom and to ensure the welfare and the care of His people and of His laborers. You won't be able to lavish enough of your possessions on Him. See how this is demonstrated by the magi: They came to worship bearing gifts.

You can almost measure a person's worship of God by the gifts he or she gives to Him for His work and for His children. Watch how you spend your money and examine what you give this year to His work. You'll be able to see what is most dear to your heart. If the furtherance of His kingdom and the need for workers in His harvest-ready fields is foremost in His heart, won't His worshipers share the same concerns?

And what will this kind of worship bring? The deep, abiding joy we all long for. Does not His Word tell us that in His presence there is fullness of joy (Psalm 16:11)? O Beloved, as you practice His presence, as you submit to His leadership, as you give to Him freely, you will sense the sweetness of His pleasure, and others will see His radiance.

O my Lord and God, when I think about all this, I realize how we have crowded You out of Christmas with all our going, our doing, our busyness, our preparations and good intentions. When I consider this unfortunate reality, I see that it is simply a specific example of a general life condition, the worship of the creature rather than the Creator. O Lord, teach me to see that time with You is a necessity. Help me to make leisure time in Your Word, in Your presence, and in prayer and adoration a priority. I want to see this habit as my reasonable service of worship so that I might know Your will in every aspect of my life.

In His Presence Is Fullness of Joy

All that I have, You have given me, and it is not mine but Yours to be used as You direct. So may I give generously, knowing that when I do so, I am giving to You.

Father, I want to relish the gift of Your Son day after day, for He truly is my life. I love You. Help me to adore You more and more, to be consumed by Your love.

Matthew
2:13-15

Now when they had gone, behold, an angel of the Lord appeared to Joseph in a dream and said, "Get up! Take the Child and His mother and flee to Egypt, and remain there until I tell you; for Herod is going to search for the Child to destroy Him." So Joseph got up and took the Child and His mother while it was still night, and left for Egypt. He remained there until the death of Herod. This was to fulfill what had been spoken by the Lord through the prophet: "Out of Egypt I called My Son."

Thirteen

Don't Miss the Picture— It's Out of Egypt

In the world, but not of the world.

This is what Jesus would discuss with His Father concerning those who believed in Him. Although they would be left in the world, He wanted to be sure they would be protected from the evil one. "They are not of the world, even as I am not of the world" (John 17:14).

If ever there was a metaphor for the world in Scripture it would be Egypt. The drama of Exodus opens with the plight of God's people living in bondage, slaves to a cruel Pharaoh who has no regard for the God of Israel—that is, until God hears the cries of His enslaved people, remembers His covenant with Abraham, and delivers them from slavery and the dominion of Pharaoh through the blood of a Passover lamb. Could it be that Matthew, under the inspiration of the divine Spirit, applied the text of Hosea 11:1 to the Son of God because of the similarities between Egypt's total disrespect for God and His people and the world's same disregard? Matthew tells us God called Joseph's family out of Egypt "to fulfill what had been spoken by the Lord through the prophet."

Why then did God send His Son to Egypt if only to call Him out? Joseph could have taken his family to any number of other places to escape the murderous Herod. Could God have wanted us to see something in a way we wouldn't forget?

Was not Jesus man? Was He not God in man, the Word made flesh, that He might be tempted in all the ways that we are? Is He not the One whom we are to follow, to imitate by walking in the Spirit even as He did, not yielding to the temptation of the devil?

Yes, my friend. Jesus was God's Son called out of Egypt— this picture of the world—for this reason: It was time to do the work of the Father. The work of the Father was to purchase our redemption through His blood that we might no longer be slaves to sin. Are you getting the picture, Beloved?

The picture is for us: God has called us, like His Son, "out of Egypt," that is, out of slavery to the prince of this world and all the world's trappings, so that we can do God's work. As He freed Israel through the blood of the Passover lamb, He freed us through the blood of His Son. When John the Baptist beheld Jesus coming to him, was it a coincidence that he cried out to all who would hear, "Behold, the Lamb of God who takes away the sin of the world" (John 1:29)? No! Jesus was the Passover Lamb who, in the sovereignty and perfect timing of God, would be slain the very day Israel celebrated Passover.

We are redeemed: no longer under Satan's power, no longer slaves to sin, because the Son has set us free. Sin's power is broken by the Son of God, who was called out of Egypt! Now we, as sons of God, are to live for the One who delivered us from Satan's kingdom.

We are no longer to love the world, for the things of this world are not of God (1 John 2:15-17). God has allowed Satan to rule this place temporarily, and so the whole world—except for you and me and every other child of God—lies under the power of the evil one (1 John 5:19). But we are sons of the living God. "I do not ask You to take them out of the world," Christ prayed for us, "but to keep them from the evil one" (John 17:15).

Oh, may we see this and live accordingly. In the world, but not of the world. In the world, but out of bondage! May we stop flirting with the world, with the sins that once enslaved us, playing the adulteress as James says. "Do you not know that friendship with the world is hostility toward God?" (James 4:4). May we remember what God told Israel: "Woe to the rebellious children...who proceed down to Egypt without consulting me," and "Woe be unto those who go down to

Egypt for help" (Isaiah 30:1-2; 31:1). Our help comes from the Lord; we "shall never again return that way" (Deuteronomy 17:16). After all, we are now heirs of God and joint heirs with Jesus Christ.

Once Jesus came out of Egypt, He never returned—nor should we. Got the picture?

⁕

O Father, I've got the picture. May I put it on every wall of my home. On every mirror. Above the television. On the computer. On the dashboard of my car. May I keep it in my billfold with my credit cards. Wear it on my wrist. Stamp it on the tops of my shoes.

Keep the words before me, "Out of Egypt."

May I remember that You have left me in the world because You have a purpose for my life. As I fulfill Your purpose, remind me daily that I am not to love the world nor to allow it to govern me. May I be a trendsetter for holiness in every area of my life and in every arena You put me in.

I know this is Your will. May I actively pursue it in loving obedience, for it's in Your Son's name, the Son You called out of Egypt, that I pray.

Matthew 2:16-18

Then when Herod saw that he had been tricked by the magi, he became very enraged, and sent and slew all the male children who were in Bethlehem and all its vicinity, from two years old and under, according to the time which he had determined from the magi. Then what had been spoken through Jeremiah the prophet was fulfilled:

"A VOICE WAS HEARD IN RAMAH,
WEEPING AND GREAT MOURNING,
RACHEL WEEPING FOR HER CHILDREN;
AND SHE REFUSED TO BE COMFORTED,
BECAUSE THEY WERE NO MORE."

Fourteen

Your Security Blanket

*S*ometimes the horrors of man are *so* hard for me to understand. How can the wicked do such terrible things and seemingly get away with it? How can people tolerate, cover, or ignore their sin—or, worse still, sanction it?

I am older now, more settled in the Scriptures. I've known and walked with God for about 40 years, so when I see and hear of mankind's atrocities, I don't ask God where He was, why He didn't stop it, or why, as we read in Matthew 2, He allowed Herod to kill every baby boy two years old and younger in Bethlehem. I have learned God's character and embraced His sovereignty. Rather than question Him, I remember that I am human and He is God. He has given me His Word. It contains everything I need to know, no less or more, and therein I find confidence and peace. So I wrap myself in the security of His Word—and there I rest, curled up with truth.

When I read of what has come to be known as the "slaughter of the innocents," I am comforted by the fact that this event was prophesied by Jeremiah before Jerusalem was destroyed by the Babylonians in 586 B.C. The layers of meaning surrounding the context of this tragic prophecy amaze me.

To begin with, Bethlehem is first mentioned in the Word in Genesis 35:19-20 as the place where Jacob, who is also called Israel, buried his wife Rachel. So Rachel becomes a symbol for the Israelite weeping for her children.

Listen to the verses quoted by Matthew in the setting of Jeremiah; listen to the hope that follows pain:

> Thus says the LORD,
> "A voice is heard in Ramah,
> Lamentation and bitter weeping.
> Rachel is weeping for her children;
> She refuses to be comforted for her children,
> Because they are no more."
> Thus says the LORD,
> "Restrain your voice from weeping
> And your eyes from tears;
> For your work will be rewarded," declares the
> LORD,
> "And they will return from the land of the
> enemy.

> "There is hope for your future," declares the
> LORD,
> "And your children will return to their own
> territory" (Jeremiah 31:15-17).

The verses in Jeremiah that precede this prophecy speak of the ultimate salvation of God's people. He assures Israel, His beloved, "I have loved you with an everlasting love; therefore I have drawn you with lovingkindness. Again I will rebuild you and you will be rebuilt" (Jeremiah 31:3-4). The verses that follow the prophecy and bring Jeremiah 31 to a close give Israel her very first glimpse of the New Covenant promise—forgiveness of their sins. Let's read them together.

> "Behold, days are coming," declares the LORD,
> "when I will make a new covenant with the house
> of Israel and with the house of Judah, not like the
> covenant which I made with their fathers in the
> day I took them by the hand to bring them out of
> the land of Egypt, My covenant which they broke,
> although I was a husband to them," declares the
> LORD. "But this is the covenant which I will make
> with the house of Israel after those days," declares
> the LORD. "I will put My law within them and on
> their heart I will write it; and I will be their God,
> and they shall be My people. They will not teach
> again, each man his neighbor and each man his

brother, saying, 'Know the LORD,' for they will all
know Me, from the least of them to the greatest of
them," declares the LORD, "for I will forgive their
iniquity, and their sin I will remember no more."

> Thus says the LORD,
>> Who gives the sun for light by day
>> And the fixed order of the moon and the stars
>>> for light by night,
>> Who stirs up the sea so that its waves roar;
>> The LORD of hosts is His name:
>> "If this fixed order departs
>> From before Me," declares the LORD,
>> "Then the offspring of Israel also will cease
>> From being a nation before Me forever."
> Thus says the LORD,
>> "If the heavens above can be measured
>> And the foundations of the earth searched out
>>> below,
>> Then I will also cast off all the offspring of
>>> Israel
>> For all that they have done," declares the LORD
>>> (Jeremiah 31:31-37).

Do you see the hope, the promise? The passage not only
assures them of forgiveness of sins, it also gives Israel the
assurance that she will never cease to be a nation! Others may
try to wipe out God's people, destroy them, and drive them

into the sea, but Israel's enemies will not succeed. So there in the midst of tragedy, God holds out a promise.

Then watch what happens in Matthew 2; it is nothing short of awesome. The actual fulfillment of this prophecy concerning the slaughter of the innocents takes place in the context of the birth of Christ, the messenger of the New Covenant promised in Jeremiah 31!

Once again, tragedy and pain are surrounded by hope. What a picture of our lives, Beloved! As children of God we are not exempt from tragedy, from pain, or from trials or tests. Nevertheless, we are surrounded by, encased in, and wrapped up in the security of Jesus Christ, which is ours because of the New Covenant of grace for which He shed His blood.

Not only that, but like Joseph, we can rest assured that God will direct our steps. Our times are in His hands. God directed Joseph to Egypt when Jesus' life was in danger. Watch again how God leads Joseph; Jesus will be protected until the time God had appointed for Him to be slain for our sins. (You'll see this pattern throughout the Gospels as you study them.)

> But when Herod died, behold, an angel of the
> Lord appeared in a dream to Joseph in Egypt, and
> said, "Get up, take the Child and His mother, and
> go into the land of Israel; for those who sought the

Child's life are dead." So Joseph got up, took the Child and His mother, and came into the land of Israel. But when he heard that Archelaus was reigning over Judea in place of his father Herod, he was afraid to go there. Then after being warned by God in a dream, he left for the regions of Galilee, and came and lived in a city called Nazareth. This was to fulfill what was spoken through the prophets: "He shall be called a Nazarene" (Matthew 2:19-23).

Did you notice? *"This was to fulfill what was spoken through the prophets."* There is our security, Beloved: God's Word is true. As I have said from the beginning of this book, not one word of the Scriptures will fall to the ground; it will all come to pass. We simply must be patient—and rest. God will deal with the wicked in His time, and He will reward the righteous when His Son comes to reign in righteousness and justice.

Thank You, thank You, Father, for being a God who never changes. Thank You for the assurance that You watch over Your Word to perform it, even as I have seen in these events surrounding the birth of your Son. Thank You for constantly reminding me of how scripture after scripture has been fulfilled to the letter. It makes me

want to read the Old Testament even more—to see Your Son in the wings of eternity, preparing to come in the fullness of time, just as You promised.

Thank You for the security I find in knowing Your Word, where I can discover You as You really are, and where I learn of Your sovereignty, which brings such peace and assurance when evil seems to triumph. Help me always remember, as You say in Psalm 73, not to forget the end that awaits the wicked.

Thank You also, Father, for sending Your Son, Jesus the Nazarene. Now I understand why and how He was called that. O Father, it is just so wonderful to know Your Word. It is my security blanket; now may I wrap myself up tight in it and rest.

Luke
2:52

And Jesus kept increasing in wisdom and stature, and in favor with God and men.

Fifteen

God Never Intended for You to Be Alone

I saw him on a television program crafted to promote the gay agenda—to show two people of the same sex as a valid family unit (which, of course, is totally unbiblical) who should have the right to adopt children.

He was just a child, and I'll never forget his face nor the gravity of the words haltingly spoken by one so young. Rejected by his birth parents and numerous foster parents who kept sending him back, he shouldered the blame for being unacceptable. "It was my fault they didn't want me," he said. "I guess I just didn't know how to live with people."

The timing was well orchestrated. The little boy with the memorable face and heart-wrenching words was being interviewed as one of several children adopted by gay couples. Finally the child had found parents—two gay men—who would take him into their family and adopt him. All that mattered to him at that juncture in his young, fragile life was that he now belonged to a family with other children who had also experienced the bitter pain of rejection.

Every child who was interviewed wanted only one thing—to belong. They wanted—and needed—the security of at least one parent who loved and cared for them. To them, two parents of the same sex were better than no family at all, even if it was a little hard to explain to friends and neighbors.

God never intended for us to be alone. Family has been on our Creator's heart from the beginning. He began humanity with a father and mother (not two mothers nor two fathers). Children would follow, raised by their parents even as God "raises" us. In creating mankind male and female and telling them to "be fruitful and multiply and fill the earth" (Genesis 1:27), God has clearly shown that His intention for man is to be part of a family. I think this is why He had Paul record in the Word that every family in heaven and on earth derives its name from God the Father (see Ephesians 3:14-15). His name—*Father*—sets the tone; His name tells the story of what family should be. And the fact that every family in heaven and on earth would find its true name, its true authority, and its true character in God as Father only affirms the magnitude of family in God's eyes.

Family. It's the most important context for relationship development in our lives, for the relationships we have with our family members impact every other relationship we have. Family is the nest built by God in which we are to be protected, nurtured, fed, hovered over, and when the time comes, taught to fly and soar on our own. Family is the culture in which we grow, in which we form our values for life.

The importance God places on family couldn't be more evident than in the birth of our Savior, for although Jesus was God in the flesh, and although God was His Father, when God sent His only begotten Son into the world, He put Jesus into a family. By divine appointment, for the first 30 years of His life the Son of God would be raised in a home with a mother, father, and eventually siblings.

Speaking of Jesus, Matthew writes,

> He came to His hometown and began teaching them in their synagogue, so that they were astonished, and said, "Where did this man get this wisdom and these miraculous powers? Is not this the carpenter's son? Is not His mother called Mary, and His brothers, James and Joseph and Simon and Judas? And His sisters, are they not all with us? Where then did this man get all these things?" And they took offense at Him. But Jesus said to them, "A prophet is not without honor except in his hometown and in his own household" (Matthew 13:54-57).

Jesus, God's Gift of Hope

Matthew makes it clear that those who lived in Nazareth knew the carpenter's family. Jesus was not raised an only child, incubated from the conflict, consternation, and even possible "contamination" other siblings might bring into His life. The Son of God, the Son of Man, would not be holy by default but by design and by choice. Jesus would be tempted and tested in every way that you and I are (Hebrews 2:17-18; 4:15), and yet He would not sin. Not even in childhood.

What does such holiness look like in real life? How does it play out? We don't know, of course, because we've never seen a young child without sin live in a family of sinners. And God has not chosen to tell us these details, so we won't speculate on what God has hidden. It is enough to understand what He has revealed.

What does He reveal in this passage from Matthew 13? God wants us to know that Jesus was part of a family. Although He belonged to God, God saw to it that His Son was raised with an earthly mother. An earthly father. He was known as "the carpenter's son." He had brothers and sisters to play and talk with, and a mother at home to supervise them. His was a working-class family from a small, nondescript village. His hometown was so unimportant, in fact, that someone would ask, "Can any good thing come out of Nazareth?" (John 1:46).

Don't miss the picture. Get God's point: A family, a sense of belonging, healthy relationships, parents—one of each sex—are by design. God's design!

But let me stop for a minute. For I know that even the mention of mother or father or family causes some of you to wince in pain. You may not want to read on because more than anything else in this world, family is all you wanted, all you craved, what you begged and cried for but didn't have.

Maybe you grew up without your father or without your mother.

Maybe the person who raised you was not your natural parent, so the mention of mother and father causes you pain.

Maybe you were neglected, abused, rejected, or simply disregarded.

Maybe the mention of family evokes such terrible memories or such agonizing longing that you shy away from any discussion of the subject.

I understand, Beloved. I have heard so many heart-wrenching stories. My heart grieves for you, and so does God's. But, dear one, avoiding the subject is not the cure for the recurring pain. Rather, you need to learn what you can, resolve the pain you have experienced, and move forward in healing. God's truths have healing power. You can cry, "Heal me, O Lord," and you will be healed (Jeremiah 17:14). His Word heals. His Word delivers us from destruction (Psalm 107:20).

When we receive His healing and move forward in faith, we can become God's instrument in the healing of others. We can reverse the damage of generations past by becoming who God wants us to be and by helping others see and become what God wants a family to be.

Our model, our hope for family, can be found in the birth and childhood of God's Son.

In God's design, childhood is something to be guarded as a time to learn, to grow, to mature in a protected environment. Childhood should be safe, physically, emotionally, and spiritually, secured by unconditional love and acceptance.

Jesus had this time. His heavenly Father saw to it. God would put no premature demands on His Son. Childhood would be just that—childhood! An opportunity to grow, as the scripture says, "in wisdom and stature, and in favor with God and men." Jesus developed His relationships both vertically and horizontally. The vertical relationship—His connection with His true Father—enabled Him to handle His horizontal relationships with others and kept Him on course as the Redeemer of mankind.

Growth is not always easy. It was not easy for Jesus. His own would reject Him, but this was bearable. Why? Because He was secure in His Father's love. Jesus had a strong beginning. It was so strong, in fact, that when the time to begin His public ministry finally came, the Spirit of God enveloped Him while the Father shouted through the clouds of heaven,

"This is my beloved Son, in whom I am well-pleased" (Matthew 3:17).

At that very moment, the Kinsman Redeemer of mankind, the One who was not ashamed to call us His brothers and His sisters (Hebrews 2:11), was about to begin His ministry of rescuing the lost (Matthew 18:11). He came for those who are orphaned by sin (Romans 5:12; Ephesians 2:1-3), harbored in the world's orphanages, and living under the cruel dominion of Abaddon, king of the abyss (Revelation 9:11). He came for those whose ancestral parents were murdered by the serpent of old, who deceived them with the consummate lie: *God doesn't mean what He says. He's withholding good from you; you can be your own god!* (Genesis 3:4-5).[5]

This was the reason Jesus was born and placed into a family: so that He might taste death for every one of us, shed His blood, and thereby pay the price of our eternal redemption *so that we could come into the family of God*. His resurrection from the dead is God's testimony, His documented proof, that Jesus' mission was accomplished. This, Beloved, is what Easter is all about.

Dear one, I don't know what your childhood was like. I don't know what longing, pain, or joy these words have evoked, but I can tell you that wherever you have been, whatever your childhood was, God can "kiss it and make it better."

He will bring you into His family if you'll let Him. If you do, you can rest assured that you will never be rejected, cast

out, or put up for adoption. Once you tell God you want
Him to be your Father and you accept His Son as your Savior
and God, *you,* precious one, become part of God's forever
family (Ephesians 2:13-22). What you have missed—if
anything—will be more than compensated for in eternity to
come (2 Corinthians 4:17-18).

And what about until then? Follow God's example. If
you're a parent, carry out your responsibility in a way pleasing to God (Deuteronomy 6:1-9; Ephesians 6:4). Follow His
example. Give your child the opportunity to have the childhood God wants him to have.

If you're not a parent, find a child to adopt, literally or
figuratively. Give him a foretaste of heaven. Either way, let a
child be a child. Help him to grow intellectually, physically,
emotionally, socially, spiritually. Protect him from the world
that wants to rob him of innocence, purity, and security. Give
freely of your love, your time, your example, your wisdom.

And finally, join with God in seeking and saving those who
are lost. Share the good news so that they can be born again
into God's family (John 3). Let this be your quiet mission as
you move through life: to serve on God's adoption team, seeking the lost and telling them about the love of God (Romans
1:14-16). It's not your responsibility to effect the adoption.
God will do that (John 6:44). Your job is simply to let the
orphans of the world know that God longs to have them in

His family. He doesn't want them to perish without ever experiencing His love.[6]

If you would like to become a child of God and you haven't responded before, maybe now is your time. All you have to do is simply believe what God says about Jesus Christ. Jesus is the Son of God, who died for your sins and was raised by God from death because God accepted His sacrifice for your sins. Apart from Him, no man, woman, or child will ever have eternal life. Jesus is the only way to God. The one who has the Son has life, and the one who doesn't will never see life. Instead, the wrath of God will abide on him or her for all eternity. There is salvation in no other (John 3:36; 14:6; Acts 4:12).

If you are willing to believe this and receive Him, then simply pray and tell God so.

You might pray the prayer I included at the end of chapter six. Or you might pray, "O God, I do believe. I have learned so much about the gift of Your Son, given to us out of Your great love. I know there is no hope of salvation apart from Him; therefore, I come right now in faith and receive Him as my Lord, my God, my Savior. Thank You for receiving me into Your family, for causing me to be born again by Your Spirit. Thank You for the gift of eternal life. Now help me to live in the fullness of Your grace. How wonderful it is to call You 'Father.' "

O God, I want to renew my commitment to You. Sometimes I find it so hard to take the time to share the wonderful news of salvation with others. I get so busy, miss opportunities in my rush, or fear the rejection and scorn of others. I forget to ask You to lead me by Your Spirit, to show me when and how I ought to speak to others about You. Help me to remember that I am never to be ashamed of the gospel of Jesus Christ, for truly, as Paul wrote, "It is the power of God for salvation to everyone who believes," Jews and Gentiles. I pray that I will be guilty of the blood of no man! I realize that only You, Father, can save these "orphans," but they cannot believe in Someone of whom they have never heard. May I proclaim the name of Christ without shame, so that they might be adopted into your family and never be alone again.

Remind me of my prayer, Father—prod me by Your Spirit—so that Jesus might see the result of the travail of His soul and be satisfied. I ask this for His joy and glory. Amen.

Luke
2:42-51

And when He became twelve, they went up there according to the custom of the Feast; and as they were returning, after spending the full number of days, the boy Jesus stayed behind in Jerusalem. But His parents were unaware of it, but supposed Him to be in the caravan, and went a day's journey; and they began looking for Him among their relatives and acquaintances. When they did not find Him, they returned to Jerusalem looking for Him. Then, after three days they found Him in the temple, sitting in the midst of the teachers, both listening to them and asking them questions. And all who heard Him were amazed at His understanding and His answers. When they saw Him, they were astonished; and His mother said to Him, "Son, why have You treated us this way? Behold, Your father and I have been anxiously looking for You." And He said to them, "Why is it that you were looking for Me? Did you not know that I had to be in My Father's house?" But they did not understand the statement which He had made to them. And He went down with them and came to Nazareth, and He continued in subjection to them; and His mother treasured all these things in her heart.

Sixteen

We Must Be About Our Father's Affairs

Have you ever had to release a loved one to the calling of the Lord? Have you ever had to let someone go to be about our heavenly Father's affairs, even though His work might take your dear one far from you? Even though it may lead down a path that is hard—or dangerous?

Innumerable books are filled with accounts of people who left all to serve God. Stories of such men and women have nurtured my soul down through the years: Hudson Taylor, Andrew Murray, C. T. Studd, John Bunyan, Isobel Kuhn, D.L. Moody, Madame Guyon, John Calvin, Martin Luther. I could go on and on. Their commitment to God, their example, has inspired me to be faithful. Their willingness to leave family and friends, to suffer hardship, to endure scorn and rejection, to be separated from loved ones for long periods of time, to face the possibility of imprisonment and loss of life has inspired me to take up my cross and follow His path of service regardless of where it may lead, regardless of the cost.

Sending off a loved one with our blessing goes against our natural instincts, doesn't it? Perhaps this is especially true with our children. We want our families to stay together, to know the security of home. We want to see them, to be with them, to grow up and grow old with them and their children. It is in our nature to protect them, to shelter them. This is natural, nothing to be ashamed of. Yet a time comes, as it did in Mary's and Joseph's lives, when we must let our loved ones be about their Father's affairs.

When Simeon stood in the temple and took the eight-day-old Jesus from Mary's arms, he said to her, "Behold, this Child is appointed for the fall and rise of many in Israel, and for a sign to be opposed—and a sword will pierce even your own soul" (Luke 2:34-35). The early years of Jesus' life would be all the time she had to prepare for this pain.

Twelve years had passed since Simeon uttered his grave words. Mary and Joseph and their family had made their annual trip to Jerusalem for the feast of Passover. When they started their journey home, they assumed that Jesus was somewhere with their fellow travelers. He was 12, able to take care of Himself among friends and family, so they hadn't worried about Him.

But then, after a full day of travel, Mary discovered He was missing.

If you are a parent, you understand, don't you? Your child has gone to play, to spend the day with people you trust, but when you go to pick him up, he's not there. Your heart sinks. You look, you call, you ask, but to no avail. No one has seen him. Fear begins to grip your heart. Where could he be? You try to keep calm, try to find out where he was last seen, yet you want to panic. Maybe you do.

All Mary and Joseph knew was that Jesus was not in the caravan. And if He wasn't there, He had to be where they had last seen Him—Jerusalem.

Each step back to Jerusalem must have brought agony. Maybe recriminations of heart. Maybe words between Mary and Joseph as to why the other hadn't checked on Him earlier. We don't know. We just know Jerusalem was a long day's journey back—too long for anxious parents.

Even after they arrived, they couldn't find Him in the city. Where should they look? Who should they ask?

They searched for three days before finally finding their Son "in the temple, sitting in the midst of the teachers, both listening to them and asking them questions." Mary was every bit the distressed mother when she said to Him, "Son, why have You treated us this way? Behold, Your father and I have been anxiously looking for you."

As a mother, I'm impressed by her restraint! Jesus had been missing for nearly five days!

His reply is astonishing. "Why is it that you were looking for Me? Did you not know that I had to be in My Father's house?"

The translation of this passage is a little difficult. Some say, "in My Father's affairs." According to the New American Standard, the literal translation is "in the things of My Father." In any case, the meaning is not difficult: Jesus knew He had to be about His Father's business.

Had Mary and Joseph forgotten that first and foremost Jesus belonged to God? That He was truly God's Son, not theirs?

This is what often happens to parents though, isn't it? We give birth to our children, pour out our lives for them, nurture, feed, clothe, discipline, and educate them, and somewhere along the line we forget that God gave them to us.

God chose the exact sperm and egg to unite.

God wove them in their mother's womb.

God numbered their days from the beginning of time.

God created them for His pleasure—not ours.

Isn't it logical, then, that each of us must be about his Father's business? Although God's affairs for us are as varied as we are, the Bible is clear: Each one who belongs to God is God's workmanship, "created in Christ Jesus for good works, which God prepared beforehand so that we would walk in them" (Ephesians 2:10).

Could Mary hold on to Jesus? No. God would give her another 18 years with Him. He would return to Nazareth with His parents and be known as the carpenter's Son. He would stay in submission to them and grow in wisdom and stature, and in favor with God and with man. But when He was 30 He would leave His parents and His hometown and begin His public ministry.

The business Jesus must be about—His Father's business— would bring Him rejection, pain, scorn, false accusations, plots and attempts against his life, betrayal by one of His chosen disciples, denial by those closest to Him, separation from His heavenly Father for a time, and finally death—a death, according to the prophet Isaiah, greater than any man has ever suffered before or since.

This is what the Father had for Him, and the Son of God would do the will of His Father.

What was Jesus doing during those five days at the age of 12 when He was separated from His parents? Even though He was God in the flesh of man, He was growing in wisdom. He sat in the midst of teachers in the temple, listening and asking questions. What humility! What an example for us! How many of us have rushed into ministry before we are prepared because we have not humbly sat at the feet of teachers? How many of us have not listened and learned from men and women of God? How many of us have not taken the time to think, to formulate and ask questions that will increase our knowledge and understanding?

Have you ever pondered the fact that although Jesus was God and understood His mission—to live in the things of His Father—He did not rush into ministry? Instead, He waited until His Father moved. And when God moved, Jesus was ready. He was prepared. He understood the purpose of life: namely, that each of us is born for God's pleasure. We are here to do His will, whatever it might be and wherever it might take us, regardless of the cost.

Mary "treasured all these things in her heart," and when the time came, she and Joseph let their Son go. Although we hear no more about Joseph, we know Mary participated in her Son's ministry. She wasn't cut off from the Offspring of her flesh. And neither are we, Beloved. Even though we may be separated from our loved ones physically, prayer keeps us in touch.

Yes, Mary's soul was pierced through as with a sword when she watched evil men jeer and crucify her Son, but she also witnessed His resurrection.

Think, Beloved. Think when your soul is pierced. Think beyond the present. Think of the hope that is yours in Jesus, of the joy that will be yours in the final resurrection, even though for now pain has run you through! In the end, if you recognize that your primary purpose in life is to be "in the affairs of your Father," joy will be yours.

⌐⌐⌐

O Blessed Father, thank You for Jesus, my hope, my example. Thank You for the lessons You are teaching me from His life. Father, I, too, want to be "in Your affairs." It is so easy to get caught up in my affairs and forget why I was born, why I am living, and that someday I will stand before You and give an account for my deeds.

Father, may I hold my family, my loved ones, my friends with an open hand, realizing that You have given me these relationships with these people not so that I will clutch them to myself but so that I will encourage them in any way I can to be about Your business. May I help them, through my prayers and encouragement, to carry Your cross. May I cheer them on, rather than try to divert them from Your course.

Keep before me the glorious resurrection that is yet to come. Help me to remember that an eternal weight of glory awaits all of us who call You "Father," a glory so great that I cannot even compare it to my temporal sufferings.

Jesus, God's Gift of Hope

Remind me to stay teachable, to continue learning, to explore Your Word, to study Your precepts, to discuss them with others, and to ask questions, so that I might learn and grow more and more into Your likeness. I want to renew my mind so that I might know Your will, which is always good, acceptable, and perfect.

O Father, my heart is filled with such joy, for I know that what I am asking is according to Your Word and therefore according to Your will. I have the assurance that You will grant the petitions I've set before You in the name of Your Son, my Savior and my example.

Matthew 3:16-17

After being baptized, Jesus came up immediately from the water; and behold, the heavens were opened, and he saw the Spirit of God descending as a dove, and lighting on Him, and behold, a voice out of the heavens said, "This is My beloved Son, in whom I am well-pleased."

Seventeen

"O My Child, Do You Know How Pleased I Am with You?"

*C*an you imagine hearing the voice of God saying, "I am so very pleased with you"?

Would anything be greater than that in all of life? Would any one moment ever be so indelibly seared into your memory? Nurtured in your soul? I would treasure such words above all else and lock them in a safe place in my heart so they could never be stolen but could be pondered over and over and over.

You might think, "If I never received any other accolade in life, this would be enough." Truly it would. For these words would satisfy the deepest longing of mind, body, soul, and spirit. No other words spoken by any creature on earth or in heaven would ever satisfy like those from the throne of the Almighty. Just to hear God say, "I am so very pleased with you, My child" would bring not only a profound contentment but also an abiding sweetness to the soul.

Oh, the inexpressible peace! The unfathomable joy! The confidence! The assurance! The sense of fulfillment! The abiding satisfaction, just to know *you* have pleased the Father!

And what joy to *know* that you truly heard the words, to be free from doubt that they were merely an imagination of your heart, a delusion grown out of your desire to please

- the One whom you love and serve and call Father

- the One who rescued you from death and destruction simply because He loved you

- the One who chose you and in His time and in His way revealed Himself to you even when you were yet in sin, ungodly, and without hope—His very enemy

- the One who turned you from darkness to light, from the power of Satan to the kingdom of God, from the second death to everlasting life

- the One who granted you forgiveness of all your sins and totally absolved you of condemnation

- the One who breathed into you a life that would never end

- the One who assured you He would never leave you nor forsake you, who by His Spirit enables you to cry, "Abba! Father!"

Oh, to know with an absolute certainty you had heard Him say, "This is my beloved child with whom I am well pleased!"

The other day I found myself gripped with doubt over a book I had written called *Sex According to God.* Could I have done better? Written it more powerfully? Made it more gripping, more compelling? I had to know, because it was being sent to bookstores across the nation. Would it do the job? Was it strong enough to accomplish my purpose in writing it? I went to the phone to call my friend, a dear friend who was also employed by my publisher. She had read it chapter by chapter. But was it really good? Adequate? I craved her evaluation. I knew she'd be honest, yet I longed for her approbation, anything to relieve my anxiety. As I stood at my desk late that night, waiting for her to answer the phone, Jeremiah 17:5-8 came to my mind, and then the words, "Trust Me."

Not once, but twice, the words "Trust Me" sounded loud in my heart. Then again the words from Jeremiah 17 washed over me, bringing a holy fear: "Cursed is the man who trusts in mankind and makes flesh his strength."

Then it came again, a third time, "Trust Me."

I didn't want to, but I hung up the phone because if these thoughts were from God, I didn't want to be disobedient. Yet I longed for the confirmation of someone walking around in the skin of a man or woman. The words of another are so wonderfully audible—you don't doubt you've heard them.

But then my next question was, *What if I heard "Trust Me" because this is what I wanted to hear?*

I realized that "Trust Me" didn't mean God was saying that the book was the best I could do. Being "best" didn't matter, I reasoned, because God was greater than my inadequacies as an author. He's known for taking nothing and making something out of it. First Corinthians 1 came to my mind: God chooses the foolish, the weak, the base, and the despised of the world to nullify the things that are valued by the world. He makes Jesus to be everything, so no flesh can boast in His presence.

Again the words were there strong in my heart: "Trust Me."

Okay, Father, I thought, *I will. I will trust, but what if the words were words of my imagination? What if...*

I couldn't do another thing. I couldn't talk to man. I might miss God if I did. So I talked to my Father. I found my latest journal, which I seldom write in, and began to write. I recorded my thoughts, my fears, and my questions. Then, like Habakkuk, I waited to hear if the Lord had really said, "Trust Me." Time would tell. Although I didn't want to wait—I wanted to know now—I knew it would take time to see whether God had really said, "Trust Me" or if the thought was birthed in my imagination. Whatever the answer ultimately turns out to be, you can rest assured it will not alter my relationship with my Father.[7]

Jesus didn't have to wonder if His imagination was at work the first time He heard the Father say, "This is my beloved Son, in whom I am well-pleased." The voice that came out of the heavens was a voice Jesus had no trouble identifying. It was the timeless voice of eternity past. The voice of His Father.

Nothing in the Word tells us that Jesus had audibly heard His Father's voice since leaving heaven to be born as the Son of man. As far as we know, this is the first time in 30 years that God spoke audibly to His Son.

When you stop to ponder this in your heart, you'll see that the timing of the Father's words to His Son—as He emerged from the waters of baptism—was incredible. Jesus was baptized on the eve of His public ministry. He was about 30 years old (Luke 3:23). He came to the Jordan and asked His cousin John to baptize Him. Although John protested, saying Jesus should baptize him instead, he complied when Jesus said it was "fitting for us to fulfill all righteousness" (Matthew 3:15).

> After being baptized, Jesus came up immediately from the water; and behold, the heavens

> were opened, and he saw the Spirit of God
> descending as a dove, and lighting on Him, and
> behold, a voice out of the heavens said, "This is My
> beloved Son, in whom I am well-pleased." Then
> Jesus was led up by the Spirit into the wilderness
> to be tempted by the devil (Matthew 3:16–4:1).

Up to this point Jesus hadn't performed a single miracle.
He hadn't turned water into wine. He hadn't healed anyone
nor delivered them from demons. Yet the Father Himself said
He was well-pleased with His Son.

Jesus hadn't even yet been tempted by the devil. Yet the
Father felt compelled to open the heavens and cry out to all
present, "This is My beloved Son, in whom I am well-pleased."

Granted, God would say these words again—later—after
Jesus' temptation, after He performed miracles. He would say
it when Jesus was transfigured before the eyes of Peter, James,
and John. But to me, the staggering truth is that God said it
the *first* time *before* Jesus began any work for God.

And what does this tell us? It tells me that what pleases
God more than anything else is our intimate relationship with
Him and our total submission to His Word, His purpose, and
His timing.

What have we learned about Jesus' life on earth in this
journey of prayer to the point of His public ministry? We
learned that Jesus grew up as a carpenter (Mark 6:3), living

with half brothers and sisters who didn't have the slightest idea who He was.

We also learned, however, from His visit to the temple, that Jesus knew who He was and what He was to be about: His heavenly Father's business. Later Jesus would state His purpose even more clearly: He came to minister, to seek and to save the lost, to give His life a ransom for all.

Yet Jesus would not rush to the task prematurely. He lived according to His heavenly Father's timetable, neither pushing ahead nor running before the Father. He did what He was supposed to do as the Son of God, the Son of Man: He lived "in subjection to" His earthly parents and "kept increasing in wisdom and stature, and in favor with God and men" (Luke 2:51-52).

Jesus grew, and Jesus pleased the Father. His dependence upon His Father is so evident in Scripture. If we continued our journey of prayer through the life of Christ, you'd discover that Jesus repeatedly withdraws from people in order to spend time with the Father and commune with Him in prayer. Why? Because He simply wanted to please His Father—to speak His words, to do His work.

And isn't that also our task in this life, Beloved? To simply please the Father? There is nothing more. There should be nothing less (2 Corinthians 5:9). Oh, to be more like Jesus! This is our hope!

O holy Father, I've come to wait in Your presence. Words fail me. I'm overcome by the longing within just to know that I am pleasing to You. How I want to live in total dependence upon You, moving through life one journey at a time, and growing as You would have me grow in every experience and relationship of life.

My ambition is simply to hear the words Your Son heard from Your lips.

You know far better than I how critical it is to my total well-being to know that I bring You pleasure. Your Word makes it clear that I was created for this.

O Father, I cannot express the passion of another's heart. I cannot enter into their intimacy with You because it is so very personal. Consequently, I cannot and should not compare my heart to theirs, nor the intimacy other people share with You to the relationship You and I have.

I simply want to make sure, my Lord, that our relationship is all that it ought to be and can be at this stage of my walk with You. I so long to press on to maturity. Speak to my heart as I wait before You, my Lord, my God, my Father, my hope.

otes

1. dc Talk and The Voice of the Martyrs, *Jesus Freaks: Stories of Those Who Stood for Jesus* (Bloomington, MN: Bethany House Publishers, 1999), pp. 124-25. This is the version of the hymn text that appears in the book.

2. Warren Wiersbe, *The Bible Exposition Commentary*, Vol. 1 (Wheaton, IL: Victor Books, 1989), p. 175.

3. Josephus, *Antiquities of the Jews,* 14.10.8.

4. Read Galatians 1:15-16 carefully. This passage shows us clearly that God saves us when He wants to save us. Salvation is of the Lord. See John 15:16; Ephesians 1:3-6; 1 Peter 1:1-2.

5. Study the implications of the serpent's words in this passage.

6. Contrast Revelation 20:6,11-15 with Revelation 21:1-7.

7. A portion of the answer would come later with an outstanding review by *Publisher's Weekly,* a secular source, of all things!

Prayers and Reflections

Prayers and Reflections

Prayers and Reflections

Prayers and Reflections